Introduction.

You'd be forgiven for thinking that this book will be like many other 'diet' books, positioning a very heavily biased viewpoint in order to 'convert' you to a new, or potentially not so new, dietary method of dropping body fat.

Let's face it, the industry is littered with diet books, all with their own agenda, designed with one thing in mind. Taking your money, rather than actually addressing any of the underlying issues that have made fat loss so difficult.

My hope and intention of this book is to break the cycle and enable you to finally learn what it is that causes fat loss as well as how to apply that in a way that works for you as an individual so you never fail another fat loss attempt again.

A challenge we all face is that when attempting to drop body fat we are confronted with a plethora of conflicting information about what you should or shouldn't and need or don't need to do in order to lose fat. That conflicting information is coupled quite nicely with an endless amount of what I would call bullshit that makes it almost impossible to know what to believe, who to trust and most importantly what to actually do.

There is a very good reason for this, if you (the consumer) never understand the principle behind your goal it makes it far easier for the industry to make money off you by selling you endless methods (ways to implement the principle) all packaged up as the 'silver bullet' for fat loss.

What's even more interesting is that as science and access to information improves, which should make achieving optimum health easier, obesity is on the rise at an unprecedented rate. Which begs the question of why?

Why is it we know more about fitness, health and nutrition than ever before and yet people seem to be becoming even more clueless on fat loss?

Convenience.

As we have progressed as a society our lives have become all about convenience.

Think back to the invention of the TV, you had to walk across the room to press the button to change channel. That regressed to getting a stick to press the button, which soon became a remote and nowadays you don't even need to press buttons you can just talk to the remote!

People are obsessed, somewhat unconsciously, with doing things quickly and easily.

We created escalators so that we could get to places quicker and people saw it as a chance to stand still and still get there.

We love convenience.

Our love of convenience is coupled with a huge lack of patience. Nowadays we want everything immediately, next day delivery used to be unheard of, now it's a commonly accepted standard and if you want something a bit fancy you can even opt for same day delivery!

This drive for convenience and speed has left us in a situation where we have become inherently lazy. Not only has it made us lazy it has also allowed us to put unrealistic expectations of how fast we can achieve things.

We want everything in an instant with minimal effort and the fitness industry has tapped into this.

So much so that the basis for almost every diet or fat loss product and method isn't around actually helping you drop fat. It's all about speed. It's about fast results, often at the expense of your own enjoyment and ultimately your prospects for long term, lasting results.

This achieves two things, firstly it leaves you totally unable to maintain any results you might get and secondly it means every time you try to lose fat again you just repeat what 'worked' before thus creating an unhealthy dependency on what can only be called a 'fucking terrible method'.

It is because of this that I have written what I believe will be a vital tool in helping you finally understand fat loss, finally making lasting results and finally breaking free of that demoralising yo-yo pattern that has plagued your every attempt.

In fact, this book is written with one simple goal to make fat loss simple.

It is my intention that by the end of this book you will know exactly what is required and have all the information needed to be able to apply it in a way that works for you,

Introducing Paul Andrews

So, who is this guy, Paul Andrews, you might well be wondering, let me tell you.

I'm Paul, a Personal Trainer from the south coast of England. I haven't always been a PT but I have always been very active and sporty.
As a kid I was always on the go, possibly due to having undiagnosed ADHD but if there was a sport, I played it basically.
As a teen, I was fairly skinny, probably skinny fat in truth, and never in amazing shape. In fact, I was always the little guy who aspired to be bigger but always struggled with getting anywhere with my fitness goals. Trust me, I was given some really dodgy advice back in the day about what I needed to do to reach my goals.

I was on and off through my early twenties with my training but found a love for it as I turned 24. I then set upon a goal at the age of 27 to step on stage and compete as a physique competitor. Much to the frustration, and against the advice, of my coach I was embarking on this naturally, without the assistance of steroids.
Believe me entering into the realm of competitive body building was an eye opener to just how many of the physiques people idolise on social media are all down to anabolic assistance… steroids. Is there any wonder people struggle with self confidence when they're comparing themselves to people who forgot to mention are on gear?!

It was right at the beginning of my journey to the stage that I picked up an injury playing football, an injury that would last two years. In my naivety I made no adjustments to my diet to reflect the severe reduction in my activity and over a two year period I got pretty fat.

It was only when a friend of mine, teammate and the captain of my football team, prodded my stomach and stated I'd gotten 'comfortable' that I realised, he was right! I'd allowed myself to get way out of shape.

It was at this point I saw firsthand just how fucked up the fitness industry is when it comes to fat loss.
Before I knew it, my attempts to get in shape led me down a path of meal replacement shakes, fasting and cutting out carbs. I made a little progress but also lost all enjoyment for life.

Whilst embarking on my own fat loss journey I began doing my PT qualifications, initially with the intention of reigniting my plans to compete and ultimately helping others do the same. What happened for me was something I hadn't expected.

I fell down a bit of a rabbit hole as I learned more and more about fitness and nutrition discovering firstly how simple the principle behind fat loss is whilst simultaneously having my eyes opened to how toxic the fitness industry is due to all the horrendously inaccurate information out there.

It was at this point that I set upon a journey to simplify fat loss and rid the industry of all the bullshit that has plagued people's attempts for so long.
So much so I once got dubbed 'The Batman of Instagram' due to my vigilante style posts calling bullshit.

It was that journey I embarked on that led me to write this book, so not only can you learn from my mistakes but so you can learn firsthand exactly what fat loss is all about, so you can spot bullshit from a mile off and also make lasting progress towards your goals.

Because, after all, no one wants to lose fat simply to regain it again.

What's in the book.

This book will take you through all of the important information surrounding fat loss and fitness in general.

We will look through;

Section 1 - Calories In
- **Nutrition**, arguably the single most important element of fat loss covering;
    - Calories
    - TDEE
    - The Calorie Deficit
    - Body Types
    - Fat Loss vs Weight Loss
    - Fat Loss vs Muscle Gain
    - Body Composition
    - Macronutrients
    - Protein
    - Carbohydrates
    - Fats
    - Micronutrients
    - Supplements
    - Nutrient timing
    - Hydration
    - Tracking Calories
    - Your Metabolism
    - Set Point Theory

- Hormones
- Female Fat Loss
- Confirmation Bias
- Fad Diets
- Nutrition In Summary

Section 2 - Calories Out

- **Training,** Wildly considered the foundation of fitness, we will look at;
  - Training vs Exercising
  - Energy Systems
  - NEAT
  - EAT
  - NEAT vs EAT
  - Training styles
  - Cardio
  - Weights & Resistance Training
  - Volume, Intensity & Frequency
  - Programming
  - Rest & Recovery
  - Sleep
  - Training In Summary

Section 3 - Building Your Lifestyle.

- **Results & Mindset,** The unsung hero of lasting results is managing your mind so we will explore;
  - The 80/20 rule
  - The 'Fuck It' Button

- Progress Tracking
- Eating The Elephant
- Speed Of Progress
- Factors Of Failure
- Goal Setting
- Motivation vs Discipline
- How To Navigate Social Situations
- Results & Mindset In Summary
- Diet Culture vs the 'Anti Diet'

Section 4 - This Is Just The Beginning.
The Takeaway, After breaking it all down, here is a summary of what's important to get you off to the best possible start.

- Acknowledgments
- Recommendations

So, strap yourself in and prepare to view fitness and fat loss like never before as you unlock the key principles behind your goal.

Section 1
Calories In

Nutrition.

When it comes to Fat Loss the single most important element, in order to achieve results, is your nutrition.

What we eat plays such a significant part purely because it is what we eat that determines how many calories we are consuming and therefore if we are actually putting ourselves into a position to lose body fat.

Now, before I dig into the finer details it is worth noting that there are countless misconceptions around nutrition that all impact greatly our ability to lose body fat by essentially confusing us with pseudoscience and essentially lies about what does or doesn't cause us to gain and therefore lose fat and when you begin to peel back the bullshit you learn that fat loss, and fat gain, is actually a very simple concept and to achieve both requires one simple thing.

To manage calorie intake in line with expenditure.

So, before I even get into calories, and nutrition in detail I am going to explain to you what a calorie is and how we burn calories each and every single day so it can become easier to understand our own energy balance.

Calories.

Before I can get into this in real detail, I need you to understand one thing and one thing only.

What the fuck even is a calorie?!

So, a calorie is a unit of measurement for energy. It is as simple as that.
Now, there are some people who will tell you they don't matter, there are some people, God help them, who will claim they don't even exist?! There are other people who will claim that they are different depending on where they come from and some folk who will also have you believe that the time of day you consume them will alter their make up and how your body processes them.

I like to call these people Shitcunts. A phrase you will hear throughout this book, and one you will no doubt be familiar with if you have followed any of my social platforms.

The reason people who make these wild claims about calories fall into the category of shitcunt is simple. A calorie is simply a unit of measurement for energy.

They are all the same, like a kilo is a kilo, a centimetre is a centimetre, a mile is a mile and a mph is a mph.
To try and claim that they don't exist or alter their make up based on the conditions they are consumed is basically just a lie.

Now, don't get me wrong not all 'calories' are created completely equal, just like a mile uphill will feel harder than a mile downhill, some foods contain a lot more calories than others.

It is not the calories themselves that are the issues, much like it isn't the miles themselves that are longer uphill. It is still a mile, but it is harder work uphill.

Some foods are more calorie dense and offer less nutritional value meaning we can't eat too much of them without consuming a lot of calories and other foods are more nutrient dense and lower calorie meaning we can eat much larger quantities of these foods without consuming a lot of calories whilst also getting a lot of nutritional value too.

Foods that are more calorie dense often tend to be tastier food and typically due to the law of sods are less satiating meaning we can consume a lot of calories from little food.

Ever thought to yourself "I don't know why I gain weight so easily; I don't eat that much". Well, a common issue people make is believing food quantity and calorie quantity are much and much the same.

Imagine a 500kcal salad... it would be huge, an entire plateful, maybe have some grilled chicken, some dressing and by the end of it you would feel like you've eaten.
Now, compare that to a 500kcal donut. The donut won't fill you up and will look pretty small on the plate. Both 500kcals, both tasty but one offers a lot more nutrient value and satiety than the other.

This isn't me demonising donuts or higher calorie food, not in the slightest but I am highlighting how we can confuse food quantity with calorie quantity and perhaps why some people try to claim not all calories are the same.

Let's be clear, all calories are the same but not all foods are and that is the key thing to remember. When eating higher calorie food, especially when seeking fat loss, we may want to enjoy them in moderation so that it is easier to manage our calorie intake without constantly eating too many calories.

I personally recommend aiming for a rough split of 80/20. 80% of the food you eat should be well balanced, nutrient dense low calorie food that helps you feel full, get the nutrients your body needs and stay within your calorie requirements, The other 20% should be the traditionally more calorie dense food that you enjoy, because no diet should demand you give up the food you love and if it does, it's not a 'diet' it's a prison sentence and a recipe for failure.
I'll talk more about this 'rule' later in the book but it can be a useful way to improve not only progress and adherence but also your relationship with food in general.

So, now you understand a calorie is just a unit of measurement and all food includes calories and some foods are more calorie dense than others we can begin to explore calories from both angles.
What we consume and what we burn.

As calories are a unit of measurement for energy it is worth highlighting that not only do we consume calories in the form of the food we eat but we also burn calories in order to keep us alive.

This isn't just the calories we burn due to exercise, so let's explore exactly how we burn calories because understanding this is a key part to understanding how to be successful in your fat loss efforts.

TDEE.

What we burn each day is known as our Total Daily Energy Expenditure, often referred to as our TDEE and is made up of a number of elements.

Many people assume the calories we burn are down to our activity and that our planned exercises is what burns the most calories, but in truth this burns on average between as little as 5-10% of our total calories.

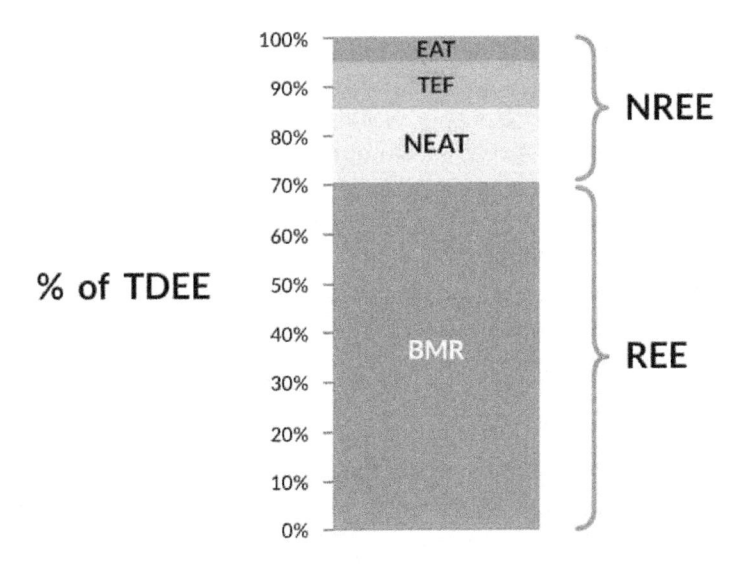

% of TDEE

- EAT, TEF, NEAT → NREE
- BMR → REE

The largest amount of the calories we burn in a day happens at rest and are burned simply by us waking up in the morning. This is known as Resting Energy Expenditure, REE and is made up of our Basal Metabolic Rate, or BMR. Around 70-75% of the calories we burn each day will be burned simply by being alive in order for our body to function and go through all the chemical processes required to sustain life.

Understanding that the majority of the calories that you burn each day will happen irrespective of if you even get out of bed can make a huge difference to the pressure you put yourself under to undertake forms of exercise that you don't enjoy. Think about it, when trying to lose fat in the past how many times have you done endless amounts of cardio or disgusting HIIT sessions because you need to 'burn fat'.
Whilst BMR will burn the majority of the calories that make up your TDEE many people believe the most important element is your planned exercise, your Exercise Activity Thermogenesis or EAT.
In fact, your EAT, or planned exercise, will actually only burn around 5-10% of your TDEE. Most people burn approximately 300-400kcal in a one hour workout, if they're lucky. The majority of people don't train every day, in fact most people train 3-4 times per week meaning the average calories burned from planned exercise over a 7 day period would be more like 171 - 228kcal per day.
When you break it down like that, it is clear to see why your planned exercise will never be the most important element of your TDEE, and why you will never out-train you're eating.

When it comes to your Non Resting Energy Expenditure there are three main components, Exercise Activity, Thermic Effect of Food and Non Exercise Activity.

The Thermic Effect of Food, TEF, refers to the calories we burn digesting the food we eat. This equates to around 10% of our TDEE.
Something that is worth noting with TEF is that the higher percentage of your diet comes from Protein, the more calories you will burn digesting food. This is because approximately

30% of the calories consumed from protein will be burned digesting it. I will discuss this in more detail later in the book.

This leaves our Non Exercise Activity Thermogenesis, NEAT. NEAT is the most important element, in my opinion, of our NREE because this is made up of all the calories, we burn each day from doing anything that isn't planned exercise, eating or at rest.

Basically, any movement you make throughout the day that isn't your planned exercise will count as NEAT. That could be mowing the lawn, hoovering, gesticulating with your hands, chewing, fidgeting, having one off the wrist and most commonly…our step count!

Increasing your daily step count is the single easiest way to increase NEAT and therefore burn more calories each day. In fact, if you can increase your protein intake and step count, you'll be significantly increasing the elements of your NREE that makes up a whopping 25% of your TDEE already! This means you can increase the calories you burn each day significantly without even setting foot in a gym!

I would argue that your planned exercise, largely due to the amount of calories you actually burn in a session, is about way more than just how many calories you burn. When we get into the training section of this book I will explain exactly why.

So, now we have looked at the total amount of calories you will burn in a day (TDEE) we can begin to look at calories from a nutritional standpoint.

The Calorie Deficit.

When it comes to fat loss there is one single principle, law of physics, that has to be present for fat loss to occur.

A Calorie Deficit. This, in short, simply means you are consuming less calories than you burn, consistently.

The trouble with the industry is that whilst there is one simple to understand principle behind fat loss, there are a million methods of creating a calorie deficit that all claim to be the key to fat loss.

What I want you to consider is the image below;

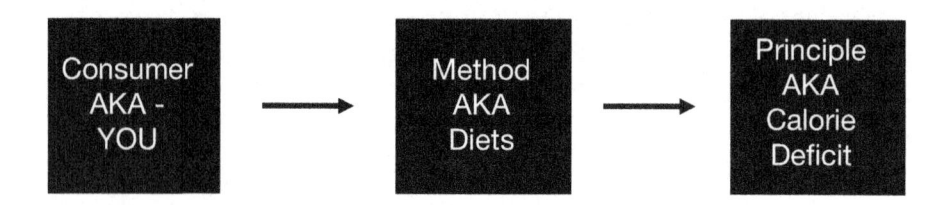

```
┌──────────┐      ┌──────────┐      ┌──────────┐
│ Consumer │  →   │  Method  │  →   │Principle │
│  AKA -   │      │   AKA    │      │   AKA    │
│   YOU    │      │  Diets   │      │ Calorie  │
│          │      │          │      │ Deficit  │
└──────────┘      └──────────┘      └──────────┘
```

On the left we have You, the consumer. On the right is the principle behind your goal and in the middle is the Fitness Industry and all the methods you cause to create a calorie deficit.

Now, you may have heard all about calorie deficits or you could be in the huge percentage of people who are hearing this for the first time and thinking "why the fuck have I never heard about this?".

It is simple really, it is very hard to make money off you, repeat income at that, if you know how the diet, programme or product actually works to create fat loss for you.

Every diet that has ever worked, every pound of fat ever lost happened thanks to the existence of a calorie deficit. How that deficit was created may vary from person to person based on their preference or the information given but the underlying reason for any ounce of fat loss is consuming less calories than you burn.

Now, most diets are largely unsustainable for two main reasons.

1) They create a way too aggressive deficit in order to generate rapid results.
2) They expect you to be way too restrictive so you could never hope to stick to them for very long.

Why?

Well, because if you get fast results, you're likely to remember that, and not how shit it was to cut out all the food you love, so the next time you want to try again you're likely to come crawling back.
The reality is the methods are often so restrictive and teach you absolutely nothing about how they work or how to maintain them meaning even if you do stick it out long enough to get results, you will have absolutely no fucking clue how to maintain them so guess what?
You go backwards.

This commonly accepted method of deception often leads to yo-yo dieting, broken relationships with food, poor understanding of general nutrition and is a significant contributor to why the vast majority of people gain back the weight lost, and often more, within 12 months of losing it.

So, what actually is a calorie deficit and how do you calculate one?

A calorie deficit simply means you are eating less calories than you're burning.

Think of it like your finances.
If you consistently earn more than you spend you will accrue wealth, much like if you're constantly eating more than you burn you will accrue body fat… to store and spend at a later date.

If, however you are spending more than you earn you will eat into those savings reducing them down.
Much like with fat loss, if you begin eating less than you're burning you will chip away at the stored body fat.

Now, if you consider fat loss like you're trying to save money, which I know is the opposite of the examples I just gave but hear me out.

If you're trying to save money you would pay close attention to the money coming in and what is going out to ensure you balance the books in favor of saving money. You won't save money every day, or even each week, but you will ensure that at the end of each week or month you are averaging the right amounts in vs out for your goal.

Fat loss is the same, you don't need to be in a deficit every single day, every single week, you just need to make sure that on average each week and month you are in a calorie deficit consistently over an extended period of time in order to drop body fat.

The reason it is imperative that you monitor what you eat rather than just trying to increase your activity is this;

If you imagine your iPhone (other phones are available, although you may be judged for your choice) If you have 100% battery and want to reduce it by 20% you would probably use some apps that you know use a lot of battery. Downloading a movie, playing a game or scrolling insta. All these apps will use up your battery bringing you down to the 80% you want to get to. However, you can use all the apps you want but if your phone is plugged into the mains, on charge, you will never reduce the battery.

Your diet is the same, you can do all the activity you like but if you're still eating too many calories you won't lose a single drop of body fat. Yes, your fitness level will improve but from a fat loss perspective you quite simply won't lose an ounce of fat.

So, given that fat loss is the result of consuming less calories than you burn, the single easiest way to ensure that is happening is to manage your calorie intake.

When it comes to the size of deficit, however, and how to apply it, that is when things can get really tricky.

The bigger the deficit the quicker the results, which in theory sounds great right? Slash calories and drop a shit load of fat nice and fast. However, the size of your deficit will determine a lot more than just how fast you lose fat.

When people claim size doesn't really matter, it's what you do with it… they may be making absolute sense when it comes to dick size but when it comes to your deficit this couldn't be further from the truth.

The size deficit you give yourself will directly impact the probability of you being able to stick to what you're doing. If you can't stick to it, you won't be making lasting progress.

I want you to imagine a scale, at one end is Speed Of Results and at the other end is Ease Of Adherence to the plan.

The closer you get to each end the further you are from the other, the faster the results the harder to adhere to it is, the easier it is to adhere to the slower results will come.
In an ideal world you want to sit somewhere in the middle with results coming quick enough to keep you interested but with the plan being easy enough to stick to so you don't quit.

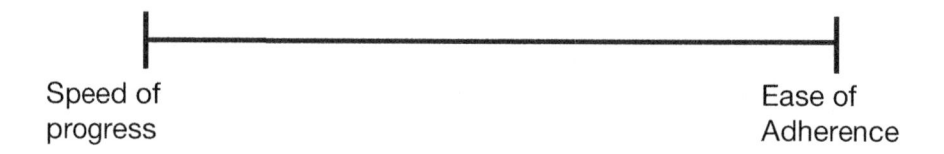

|─────────────────────────────────|

Speed of progress   Ease of Adherence

The reason why you ideally want to place yourself somewhere in the middle is because if the plan is too easy there is no actual need to stick to it and you likely will not see results because you're not actually challenging yourself. You're probably not making any actual change to your currently lifestyle, and if you're trying to lose body fat it is likely that your current lifestyle is the root cause to why you're needing to lose body fat.

Now, on the flip side of this if you make the plan too restrictive, whilst this will be excellent for progress you are very unlikely to stick to it long enough to be able to hold onto any results you achieve.

The reason for this is when you're in a calorie deficit you are consuming less calories than you're burning, calories are a unit of measurement for measuring energy. Our bodies require energy to function and our BMR is the minimum amount of energy that our body needs to complete all the chemical processes required to sustain life, also known as our metabolism.

When we create an energy deficit, we are deliberately consuming less energy than we are burning in order to burn the energy we have stored up as fat within the body.

Because, essentially, overtime we have been consuming too many calories so our bodies have been storing the extra energy for future use.

If we take the deficit too low, i.e., below our BMR, for an extended period of time, whilst it is great for fat loss it is not good for how we feel and function.
When we take calories too low what happens is we begin to feel what can only be described as shit.
We become fatigued, grumpy, have trouble sleeping, have low energy, constantly hungry, we perform worse when training, we recover worse and basically just end up feeling horrendous. You may suffer with headaches, muscle cramps, brain fog and countless other symptoms.
This is because our body doesn't have enough energy coming in to fuel us to complete the chemical processes required to sustain life, let alone our activity level.
So, to combat this our body will in short, slow us down, so we burn less calories in order to bring some balance to things.

This is NOT Starvation Mode. In fact, starvation mode doesn't exist, and contrary to what morons selling meal replacement shakes will tell you, doesn't happen if you skip breakfast, just ask the people who fucking love to get their dicks hard over intermittent fasting because that's essentially not eating breakfast.

Anyway, I digress, as our bodies slow us down what often happens, which is why people think starvation mode is a thing, is we begin burning less calories, through being less active, this is often coupled with gradually increasing what we consume by trying to get energy boosts from typically higher calorie foods for example seeking the 'sugar rush'.

When these two things are at play what often happens is we come out of a calorie deficit and back into a surplus though eating more and doing less and so we gain some fat back, often leading people to believe they're gaining fat by eating too little.

It is a common misconception around the difference between calorie intake and food intake, you can consume a large number of calories from a small amount of food, just the same as you can consume a small number of calories from a large amount of food depending on what you're eating. There is a distinct difference between calorie dense food and nutrient dense food, just look at 400kcals of salad vs a 400kcal doughnut.

Now, this isn't me shitting on doughnuts and saying only eat salad, because let's face it the best salads are the ones that have a lot more than just salad to them, like chicken, pasta and sauces.

So, you're probably wondering what size deficit you should be aiming for in order to lose fat but not end up feeling like a bag of dicks.

This isn't a completely straight forward process, it's a calculation that needs to be done for each individual based on a number of factors, however a general rule of thumb is once you know your TDEE to subtract around 350-500kcal off of that amount and start there.

Some people might be able to go slightly more aggressive and feel good still, others will need a little bit less to function well and not feel horrendous.

Equally, women going through menopause, suffering with PCOS or thyroid issues, for example, may need a slightly larger deficit to account for the fact they burn less calories at rest than the general population. I'll cover more on this later.

What I would say is to really know if it is working for you is to give yourself a good amount of time to track progress. Don't do it for one week and expect insane results and then slash calories if you haven't had just that.

I would stick to it for a few weeks, tracking measurements each week, weight once a month, and adjust by a small amount if you haven't seen any progress in three or four weeks, try that for a few weeks and adjust again.

One thing to consider, however, before you adjust calories is are you tracking your intake accurately and are you actually burning as many calories as you think.

This is because the three main reasons people don't see progress when in a deficit are;

1) They're underestimating how many calories they're consuming
2) They're overestimating how many calories they're burning
3) They're not being patient enough.

If you can hand on heart, say your tracking accurately and you're working as hard as you say you are and you're still not seeing progress, and it's been a good few week's, it might be worth making a small reduction to your calories and following that for another few weeks to see what the results are.

Something a lot of people make the mistake of doing is changing too much at once so they have no idea what change worked but they also have fuck all chance of sticking to the changes if they're too drastic.

People get bogged down with the method they're going to adopt to create the deficit that they overlook the likelihood of actually sticking to it long enough to get results.

It is also incredibly common for people to focus and fixate on the wrong elements when trying to lose body fat which more than often leaves them wondering why it isn't working and all too often feeling like they're the problem.

Sound familiar? You're not alone there at all. Perhaps this will sound familiar as well;

Most people, when they want to lose body fat assume that simply joining the gym will be the solution to their problems. However, it is not what you do for an hour in the gym 3 times per week that will change your life, it's what you do for the other 165 hours of the week that will determine your success.

If you had a leak in your bathroom, the place is knee deep in water, you might think grabbing a bucket and throwing water out the window would be incredibly helpful. However, if you haven't stopped the water flooding into your bathroom, you're quite literally wasting your efforts.
We already covered how training equates to around 5% of the calories you burn each day so if you're purely focusing on training alone as a way to burn fat, you're setting yourself up for disappointment.

Similarly focusing on cutting carbs, removing sugar, eliminating, or avoiding any kind of food from your diet simply to lose fat is also not the answer.

Yes, cutting meals down by one, by not having breakfast can help create a deficit. Just the same as cutting carbs our can too. But if the idea of doing it isn't something you can see yourself doing long term as a lifestyle it really isn't the right approach for you.
Some people fucking love not having breakfast, some people will hate the idea!
Life is like that, so many things come down to preference and if it's not your preference I would always recommend avoiding it because there's more than one way to create a deficit and finding a way that works for you is the key to long term success.

Whilst some of the fad diets out there might promise rapid results that are significant, I am sure we have all seen the false promises of losing 10kg in a month.
The thing with fad diets is that they're just like putting a plaster over an axe wound.
Whilst it may initially appear to be working, that plaster will eventually become saturated and fall off, because if you have a gaping wound in your leg, you actually need stitches, not a plaster.
If you're not addressing the underlying issues with your diet, you will never actually achieve lasting results.

In order to lose fat and more importantly maintain it you need to address the issues that caused you to gain fat in the first place.

Fat gain comes from eating more calories than you burn consistently over an extended period of time, this is born out of, usually, not understanding how many calories your body actually needs.

That is then exacerbated by people adopting very short-term quick fixes that are incredibly unsustainable in an attempt to lose fat.

Often, they lose some but can't stick to their chosen method and quit, or they reach their goal but have absolutely no idea how to maintain it, because they haven't attempted to address their relationship with food and end up going backwards.

It is one of the main reasons why almost 90% of people who lose fat end up gaining it back, and often more so, within the first 12 months.

If you can understand how many calories you require, how to then apply that to a lifestyle that you actually enjoy and feels as least like a diet as possible the sooner you will not only make progress but also maintain it.

Because, after all, it is significantly easier to maintain your results when all you're doing is gradually bringing your calories back up to maintenance, rather than completely changing everything about how you eat and your activity level. The less disruption to your everyday lifestyle the more likely you are to make progress and be able to keep hold of it.

The easier you find something, the more likely you are to actually do it.

Now, whilst calories are absolutely king and the single most important element to your progress there are other elements to your nutrition that you will want to focus on, or at least pay attention to that will help you along the way.

But before I go balls deep into all thing's nutrition, I am going to explore a few topics that often make life difficult when it comes to fat loss.

Body Types.

Body types, or as they're officially known Somatotypes are a group of three categories that people can be placed into depending on their body shape.

The three body types are;

Ectomorph,
Mesomorph,
And Endomorph.

The concept of these three body types was a first theorized in the early 1940's by W.H Sheldon as a way to categorise people based on their body shape.

These three body types or body compositions were believed to be predetermined and as such people were confined to which ever body type, they had.

The characteristics of the three body types are as follows;

Ectomorphs are traditionally very lean and slight, typically tall and thin. Gangly if you will.
A Mesomorph would be someone who is also lean in appearance but with a more muscular frame with broader shoulders and a narrow waist.
Lastly, endomorph would be anyone who was carrying a lot of body fat, usually centered around the middle.

Even to this very day when doing GCSE PE and your level 2 and 3 PT qualifications you will be taught all about body types. There are even coaches out there who have built their entire business model on the concept of 'body types'.

What is strange about this is that almost as soon as the concept was first theorized it was discredited when it was highlighted that through training and nutrition you can change your body shape, body composition and therefore move from one 'type' to another meaning our body types aren't predetermined and in short, the idea of body types doesn't actually exist.

Despite this there are a plethora of people out there who will have you believe the key to your goals is either eating or training for your 'body type' I like to call these people, you guessed it… shitcunts. The reason why body types is still even in the conversation is because people will do just about anything to make themselves sound knowledgeable and to add gravitas to what they're saying in order to sell you a product or service. More often than not that you don't even fucking need.

Body types creates an air of mystery and therefore creates a demand. If someone suggests you're not reaching your goal because you're not training or eating for your body type, you're likely to question;
"What even is my body type?" Now, if they can not only help to confirm your body type and sell you a plan based around that body type it is bound to sound compelling. That is until you realise body types aren't a thing and therefore, they're deliberately misleading you in order to make money off you.

So, Somatotypes, body types, quite simply aren't a thing and you don't need to base your training or nutrition around what body type you are.

Fat Loss vs Weight Loss.

Something that people often get confused is the difference between fat loss and weight loss. Whilst there is a correlation between the two, they're not intrinsically linked and don't coexist in perfect harmony. In fact, it is perfectly possibly to achieve one without the other in both cases.

In fact, I would say fat loss and weight loss are like the two people who aren't in a relationship but each time they're out drinking together, end up fucking each other. They operate entirely independently of each other but now and then you can find them hooking up, but they're definitely not mutually exclusive.

We can lose fat without losing weight and we can lose weight without losing fat. In truth, it is very easy to lose weight without losing fat.
This is largely in part to the fact out body weight is made up of a lot more than just how much fat we have.
Our body weight is out total weight including;
Our bone density,
Total body water,
Muscle mass,
Fat mass,
How much food is in our system,
Our organs & skin.

Basically, everything that makes us contributes to our weight and our weight is, in reality, simply our gravitational pull, our relationship with gravity and the ground.

There are a number of factors that can influence our weight on a daily basis that can cause the scales to go up and down, often by significant amounts. Which, when you're trying your hardest can be incredibly confusing and frustrating.

Our weight can be easily influenced by;
How much food is in our system,
How well hydrated we are,
How many carbs we ate the day before,
How much salt we consumed the day before,
Fibre intake,
If we have been for a shit,
Hormonal fluctuations.

All these factors can cause the scales to go up and down and have nothing to do with body fat. And yet our weight is the single biggest metric people use to gauge their performance when fat loss is the goal.

What is even more strange is when you actually break down a 'weight loss' goal no one actually cares about how much weight they lose, they want to lose fat and change their body composition. To prove this, I will pose a question with two options. A quick game of would you rather;

If given the choice, would you rather to be 10kg heavier than you are now with a physique you love or 10kg lighter than you are now with a physique you dislike?

In all my years of coaching, I have never had someone opt for option 2. Why? Because when it all comes down to it weight loss isn't the actual goal. Changing how you look and feel is.

If it was purely about weight loss there are a number of rapid fixes you could adopt to achieve this, I have taken the liberty of listing some below;

Taking a massive shit,

Food poisoning - *I once lost 11kg in 8 days thanks to this!*
Only putting one foot on the scales,
Cutting off a limb,
Chopping off your head,
Cutting out eating indefinitely.

If weight loss is the only goal, then all of the above will do the trick very well. In fact, the only times I would ever say you need to focus on just losing weight would be if you're a fighter trying to make weight for a fight or you're doing a sky dive and need to be under a certain weight for the parachute to work.

Outside of those two scenarios the goal is never about strictly weight loss.

It is always about fat loss. Now, because body fat only makes up a small portion of your body weight it is not uncommon to lose fat whilst the scales barely move, or heaven forbid, go up!

A great way to measure fat loss is to track measurements around key areas, this is because if you're a physically smaller human being you're losing fat, even if the scales haven't budged as you might have liked!
As well as that take good look in the mirror, at how your clothes fit because if your clothes are looser, you look like you've lost weight then that's also a great indicator of progress.

One of the biggest mistakes people make when wanting to lose fat is they focus entirely on their weight and even set a goal weight. Often saying things like *"I'll be happy when I get down to *insert weight here*"* the reality is this…

Almost everyone who has said that has either never reached the goal weight or when they got there still hated what they saw because they didn't look how they wanted to look when they reached the weight.

If you're watching the scales week on week, some people day to day and occasionally for some people multiple times per day you will see your weight fluctuate, A Lot! It will go up and down like a whore's underwear. That is totally normal but if you're focusing on it, needing it to move in only one direction, to bring you happiness, and looking at it every 5 minutes I have bad news… You will feel pretty shit about your progress because, much like the rising of the sun, we can guarantee our weight will fluctuate every single day.

My advice is this, if you wish to see what your weight is doing, check it once per month, you'll notice the downward trend without needing to analyse all the fluctuations. Check your measurements each week or every two weeks and you're far more likely to see progress week on week keeping you feeling more positive but I will cover tracking progress later in the book in more detail.

Something we all need to appreciate when it comes to fat loss is this very important point;

We can't spot reduce where we lose fat from!

Despite what some cunts will tell you with their 'belly fat busting' diets and workouts, their bingo wing workouts and any other claims suggesting you can target fat loss from a specific area, the fact is we can't pick and choose where we lose fat from and how fast it comes off each area.

What you can do is reduce calorie intake to create a deficit, be consistent and patient and watch the results follow.

Why can't we spot reduce? Firstly, because it doesn't work like that. Whilst we can target where we grow muscle through training we can't target where we lose fat from.
So those crunches you're doing for a flat stomach are a bit of a waste of time.

The reason for this is simple.

Imagine your body is a swimming pool. If that pool is full (your body fat) and you want to let the water out in just one corner. The only way to do that is to fully isolate that corner, block it off then empty it. Because all the time it is part of the entire pool the water will only be reduced across the whole pool and not that one corner. Even if that's the corner you use a bucket to take water from!

You can put more plugs into the pool in different areas too but that won't change the fact the total water will reduce.

Your body is the same, the only way to only lose fat from a specific area is to cut that area sway from your body… shocker that you won't be doing that!

So, for fat loss, even in specific areas, you have to manage your calorie intake into a sensible deficit and be patient as well as consistent!

Fat Loss vs Muscle Gain.

Another element people often struggle to get their head around is if they should be aiming to lose fat or build muscle. It is possible to do both for sure but often makes sense to prioritise one.
If this sounds like you then ask yourself one simple question;

Do I have fat to lose?

If you answered yes to this, I would start there. Start with fat loss because unless you drop body fat and reduce your body fat percentage it is harder to see how much muscle you actually have.

This doesn't mean just doing cardio and sacking off any resistance training or any behaviours that will elicit muscle growth. Quite the opposite in fact. Regardless of the goal I would recommend adopting a plan or lifestyle that includes resistance training for a number of reasons, many of which will be covered later in the book.
But in truth when it comes to building muscle or losing fat, the routines can be identical from a training perspective all that really changes is the amount of calories required for each goal.

For fat loss, as we now know, we need a sensible and sustainable calorie deficit.
For muscle growth we need a small, much smaller than most people realise, calorie surplus. This is because to grow new muscle we need additional calories to fuel the recovery as well as growth of new muscle tissue.

It is essentially the opposite of dropping body fat. What we don't want to do is take calories too high though. Most people

go full blown *'Bulk Hogan'* and eat everything in sight for the gains and just end up adding body fat.
Building muscle takes time and the longer you take to add size the leaner the mass you will add.

There are some other subtle differences between losing fat and building muscle. I like to highlight these visually with what I call the pyramid of importance.

Pyramid of Importance For Fat loss.

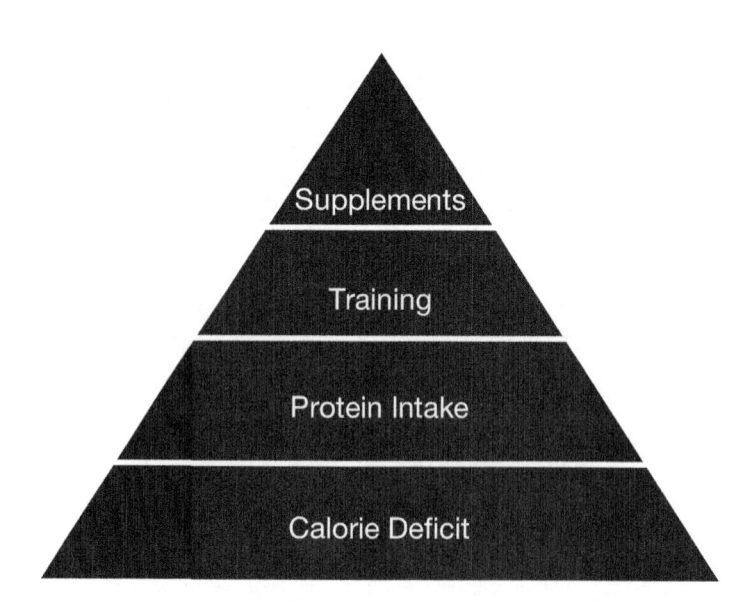

As you can see, the foundation of fat loss is the calorie deficit, without this nothing happens. Secondary to this we have the need to get good protein in, then we need a good activity level, ideally including resistance training and lastly, if you're struggling to get enough of the right nutrients or protein etc. then it might be worth exploring some supplements to help. Yes, there is more to it, like good sleep, hydration, rest and recovery etc. but if you prioritise your efforts like this you will make progress.

Pyramid of Importance For Muscle Gain

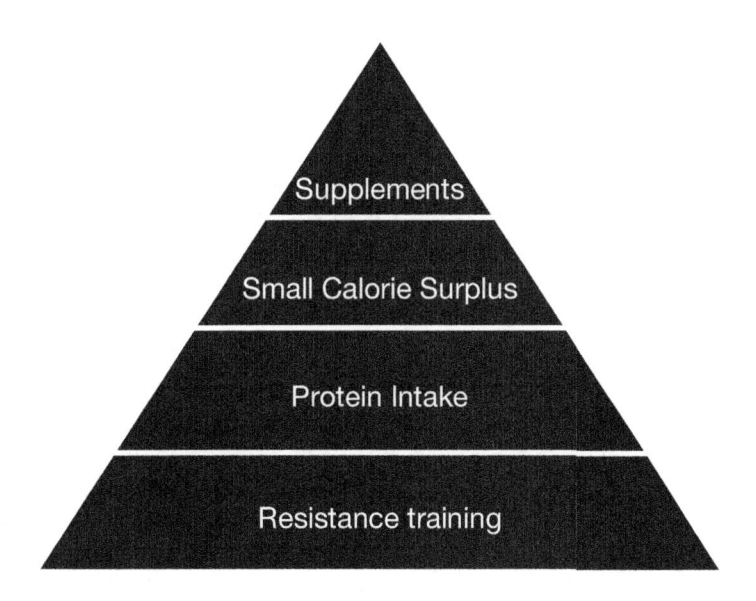

Pyramid from top to bottom: Supplements / Small Calorie Surplus / Protein Intake / Resistance training

With a muscle growth goal, the foundation is the training. Without the correct stimulus you simply can't grow muscle. I'd love to say you can just follow the bullshit you see on social media, simple home workouts, bodyweight stuff, go keto, do the carnivore diet etc. but the reality is, without the correct stimulus you won't elicit growth.
For muscle growth you need to fatigue the muscles, causing tears to the muscle fibre that through a combination of the right rest, protein and calorie intake will result in the growth of new muscle fibres.

Now, you could argue that calories are the second most important element but in truth I would say it's protein because if you train hard and get the right amount of protein it will be far more beneficial than just eating a small surplus as we need the protein to stimulate the repair, recovery and growth of new muscle.

Now, what if you wanted to achieve both fat loss and muscle growth at the same time, is it even possible?

In short, yes, it is possible but growing muscle in a deficit takes a very long time. Which is why I would always recommend focusing on one thing at a time to avoid any disappointment or frustration with progress.
So, with that in mind if you're still wondering should you lose fat or build muscle ask yourself this;
"Do I have fat I need to lose?" If the answer is yes, start with aiming to lose fat. Still include resistance training and a high protein diet but focus on losing the fat and once you're leaner and you can see what you're working with you can begin to build muscle from there. It's easier to build muscle and change our body composition from a leaner standpoint not least in terms of being able to see your progress.

Which brings me nicely onto the next section of the book which is looking at our body composition.

Body Composition.

I've already posed this question once but, let's just double check here;
If I gave you a choice of being 10kg heavier than you are today with a physique/ body shape you absolutely love or being 10kg lighter than you are today with a physique that isn't much different to the one you have, or is one you don't love… Which would you choose?

I can almost guarantee that each and every one of you reading this opted for option one.

Why? Because when we look and feel fucking amazing, we don't really give a shit about what we weigh.

Many people set a goal weight hoping to feel happier when they reach it but in their head is a picture of how they want to look, not what they want to weigh and often the two don't fully align. This is largely down to the fact our body composition is key to our perception of how we look and the progress we're making.

So, what is our body composition?

In short, our body composition is the make-up of fat vs muscle we hold.
We have already explored that our weight is more than just how much fat we have and our body composition emphasises this.

You could have two people the same age, height and weight with vastly different body compositions.

You could have two guys who're 5'10 and 15 stone, you'd be forgiven for assuming they're overweight, borderline obese in fact. But here's the thing one of them could be a body fat percentage of 8% and carrying a phenomenal amount of muscle mass, the other… could be around 30% body fat and the two would look very different.

Same age, height and weight so therefore the same BMI but vastly different compositions. Just one of the many reasons why BMI is largely bullshit. Sure, there is a correlation between age, height and weight for optimum health but given the example above it shows how it's pretty flawed and there's more important things than BMI for gauging health.

Now, back to body comp!

So, there are a number of things people believe about body composition that aren't true and I am about to clear this mess up for you, so buckle up!

Muscle weighs more than fat! - Wrongo! It weighs the same 1lb of fat weighs the same as 1lb of muscle just like 1kg of feathers weighs the same as 1kg of bricks. But muscle is a lot more dense than fat meaning it takes up less space, which is where the confusion comes from. This is why those who have more muscle and less fat can weigh the same as someone with less muscle and more fat who would appear much 'larger'.

Fat is relaxed muscle? - Again, this just isn't true, fat and muscle are two entirely different things. Muscles don't 'relax' and turn to fat. Muscles that aren't utilised break down and are lost, they lose size and strength but they don't turn to fat. Often, though, the space vacated by muscle is then filled by fat cells which is where the illusion of muscle 'becoming' fat comes from.

You can turn fat into muscle! - Sorry, this again is bollocks. You can't turn fat into muscle just like muscle doesn't turn into fat. The two are totally different. When people believe they are turning fat into muscle what they are doing is known as body recomposition. This is the process of losing fat and building muscle independently of each other over time. Much like what I said above, this creates the illusion that fat has 'turned into' muscle but in truth fat cells have been reduced in size through caloric restriction and the space left has been filled by lean muscle mass to alter the aesthetic look to appear as though the fat was turned into muscle.

In summary focusing on improving body composition in order to achieve the aesthetic look you are after is far more important than worrying purely about what you weigh.
Being able to add more muscle whilst losing fat is a great way to focus on improving your overall health without becoming a slave to the scales.
It is also worth noting that it is possible to reduce your body fat percentage without losing body fat.

Wait!! What did he just say?!
Yes, hear me out. If you grow muscle, so bring yourself into a surplus and your start point is around 20% body fat, by adding more muscle you won't have lost any fat but if you add 5% more muscle mass your body fat percentage will have reduced. It's the same amount of fat mass in terms of weight but as an overall percentage it will mean your body fat percentage has reduced.
This is another reason why it may be beneficial, when there is fat to lose, to focus on fat loss first of all. It is also another reason why body fat percentage isn't wholly accurate for indicating progress.
That and the fact that to accurately calculate body fat percentage you would actually need to undergo an autopsy

which isn't exactly an ideal way of finding out your body fat percentage as you'll be dead.

Sure, you can use some fancy scales, calipers or other techniques to calculate body fat percentage but they are only about 80% accurate. At best!

The best indicator of body fat and overall body composition is what you can actually see. You will be able to see if you're getting leaner, adding more muscle and therefore improving your body comp without needing to know the exact ratio of muscle to fat percentages.

In fact, the 'percentages' of each is a bit like your weight… irrelevant if you like what you see, so focus on the behaviours that will elicit the result you are after and be consistent with that rather than getting obsessed and bogged down with the numbers associated with the result you're after.

Now we have covered all of this, let's take a deep dive into nutrition in detail and explore all that makes up our food and our diet, starting with something I am sure you have all heard mentioned a million times… Macros!

Macronutrients.

Now whilst calories, and managing your calorie intake in particular, is absolutely the key to your success when it comes to all things fat loss there are some other elements to your nutrition that will also help you along the way.

In this section of the book, I will talk you through macronutrients, the role of them in your diet and what is and isn't important to monitor when it comes to your progress.

So, first of all, what even are macronutrients?

When it comes to nutrients our body needs a mix of micro and macronutrients. Micronutrients being the vitamins and minerals that we need to function in typically low quantities (more on this later on) and macronutrients, or macros, are the nutrients we need in much larger quantities.

Our Macronutrients are made up of three food groups, that everything we eat will contain in some quantity.
Those three food groups are;
Protein,
Fats &
Carbs.

I will discuss each one of these in more detail individually but you may well be aware of them and potentially for all the wrong reasons.

In the fitness, particularly diet industry Carbs and Fats have had their reputations tarnished by many a diet approach.

For a long time, fat was demonised and the concept of going Low Fat was hailed as the key to fat loss. This approach, in fairness, can be a helpful way to create a deficit because of all three macronutrients Fats carry the largest amount of calories, 9Kcal per gram to be precise. So, by restricting fat from your diet, you can free up a lot of calories which can make being in a deficit a little easier.

The challenge here is fats can often be quite tasty meaning you would have to avoid some pretty nice food if you strictly went low fat with your diet.

Then there is the humble carb, or carbohydrate. These are our main energy source but sadly due to the emergence of the Keto diet they are demonised by many when in truth, they're not only essential for energy & low in calorie they are also fucking delicious.

They're also only 4Kcals per gram so more than half the calories of dietary fats.

Lastly, we have Protein, the only macronutrient that hasn't been completely slagged off by diet culture and in truth arguably the most important macro of the bunch.

Much like Carbs, protein is also only 4kcals per gram and bring a multitude of benefits to your diet.

It is because of this that we will start off by looking at protein in the most detail.

Protein.

So, protein, after your calorie intake is probably the second most important element of your diet, for so many reasons. Firstly, we have the fact that protein is essential for muscle repair, recovery and re-growth. Now a lot of you may well be thinking that your goal is fat loss, you don't care about growing muscle, but hear me out here.

When you bring yourself into a calorie deficit you will be consuming less energy than you are expending, a knock-on effect of this is a reduction in muscle mass, which may not sound like a bad thing but when you consider that the more muscle you hold the more calories you burn at rest it is clear to see why we would want to hold onto as much muscle as possible.

Because, after all, the more calories we can burn at rest the easier being in a deficit will be but also the less pressure there is to burn calories from activity so holding onto as much muscle as we can, will make the process of losing fat much easier!

Not least because for most people the goal isn't just about losing fat it is about having a physique, they're proud of that gives them confidence and if you just lost fat, and muscle, my guarantee is you would end up with a physique that you aren't totally happy with.

To put it into perspective if you compare a long-distance runner's physique to that of a 100m sprinter their physiques are very different.
This is down to how much muscle they hold, long distance runners tend to be very slight, with no real shape to their bodies, because carrying too much muscle will be detrimental

to performance whereas the sprinter needs to be more explosive so holding more muscle will help them be more powerful and therefore run faster over short distances.

But if you were to ask people, who are wanting to lose fat and improve their overall physique, which physique they would like to create most people would opt for the more athletic physique of a sprinter.

In fact, a mistake a lot of people make is losing a lot of weight without prioritising resistance training and adequate protein leaving them with a physique that, albeit is smaller than they were, doesn't give them the aesthetic look they're after. Most people wait until this happens before they begin prioritising muscle.

Now, if they focused more on protein and resistance training whilst in a fat loss phase, they would be able to change their overall body composition as well as drop body fat.

Another significant advantage of protein is its thermic effectiveness.

When it comes to burning calories at rest, we will burn 30% of the calories we consume from protein just to digest it. This means if you eat a high protein diet not only can you ensure you hold more muscle meaning you improve your overall physique and burn more calories at rest but you will also have a more thermic-effective diet meaning you burn even more calories at rest.

Due to its thermic-effectiveness, protein also is the most satiating food group meaning not only does it serve to burn more calories at rest but it also keeps you feeling fuller for longer, something that can really help making being in a deficit infinitely easier!

After all, no one wants to be hungry all the time!

Whilst all of the above is great for adhering to a deficit and enhancing your chances of success one of the other significant benefits of protein is how it is used by the body to assist with muscle recover, repair and regrowth.

The more muscle we hold the more calories we burn at rest, if we throw resistance training into the mix we will burn even more calories at rest, all very helpful with trying to adhere to a deficit. However, when in a deficit it is entirely possible, especially for those doing drastic fad diets in huge, unsustainable defats, that you will lose muscle as well as fat.

In order to prevent this keeping protein high is essential as not only does it do all the good stuff, I just told you but it also allows us to preserve existing muscle, as well as aiding the repair and recovery of our muscles and promotes the growth of new muscle too!

The way our body uses Protein falls into two categories, Muscle Protein Synthesis (MPS) and Protein Synthesis (PS) Now, when we talk about protein and the absorption rate many people believe that only MPS occurs when we consume protein.
When it comes to MPS our bodies will be able to absorb and distribute around 35-50g of protein direct to the muscles in any one go. This will vary person to person, some will be slightly more some may be slightly less but own average somewhere between 35-50g in one sitting will be delivered direct to the muscles.

The trouble is many folk in the fitness industry believe that the rest is just wasted. In fact, a lot of PT's even are taught that if you have more than 50g in one sitting the rest is just pissed out as waste.

I have news for you, if you have protein in your piss… you're in trouble, that liver and those kidneys of yours are in a bad way.

We don't piss out what isn't sent straight to the muscles, we digest it and it is distributed round the body for use as energy etc. This is Protein Synthesis; it is the process of the body absorbing and using Protein aka calories as energy.

Plus, when you take into account all of the thermic-effective benefits, the satiating impact of protein, there is way more benefit to eating more of it than just becoming Lord Swoldermort.

People, however, for years have just been led to believe that protein is just about getting jacked and adding huge amounts of muscle. The reality is most of the physiques we look at that are fucking huge, whilst they may claim they're just using weigh protein and lifting weights are almost certainly on gear too!

Simply eating protein won't make a person big or pack on insane size, believe me, if it was that easy I, and many others like me, would have had a much more enjoyable training life and would be twice the size we are!

The long and short of this is this, get your protein in! You need between 1.5-2.2g per kilo of bodyweight each day on average. The best way, if you want most of that to go direct to your muscles is to get it in little and often through the day where possible.

In terms of where to get it from there are so many options here, those who eat meat can enjoy the fact that meat and dairy products are a great source of protein. Lean cuts of white meat are the lowest calorie source usually boasting the best calorie/protein per gram so turkey breast and chicken breast are absolute winners.

Eggs are good as well, the whites is where the protein resides so if you're worried about calories then leave out some yolks and you're golden. But to get your protein in it's not all about chicken breast and eggs.
Red meat & fish are excellent sources that are packed with other nutrients, vitamins and minerals too that make them a great source of protein, whilst slightly higher calorie they are a valuable option.
You then have cheeses too, who doesn't love cheese?! But as good as cheese is for protein it is going to be higher calorie so be mindful of this. That being said there are some great very low-calorie high protein cheeses out there now meaning you can boost that protein, eat the cheese and not hammer the calories.
Lastly there's your cottage cheeses and yoghurts that can come in fat free options and still boast a large amount of protein per 100g.

But what about if you don't eat meat, I hear you say?
Well pulses and legumes are a fantastic route too, the only thing to be mindful of is the calories, to get 100g of protein you will find you will consume more calories than if you got 100g protein from chicken for example. But as long as you manage your overall calories you'll be just fine!

There are also peas as well which won't be as high calories as pulses and legumes but may require you to eat an awful lot to actually get a large amount of protein from.

If you're struggling still, you obviously have supplements, now there will be more on this later but there is absolutely nothing wrong with using a good quality Whey protein or Plant based Whey alternative to boost that protein intake up and there are some fantastic, and low calorie, options out there that can make boosting your protein up so much easier as well as bringing a lot more variety to your diet.

Now, you might be wondering, if protein and calories are so important what about fats and carbs?

In truth, the mix of these two macronutrients is practically irrelevant if you're consistently managing calories and protein. In fact, studies have shown that there is no difference in results of those going high carb or low carb, high fat or low fat when calories and protein are matched and kept consistent. Which means the make-up of carbs and fats is largely down to your personal preference. Good news if you love carbs and were considering doing Keto because some zealot cunt had you believe carbs are the devil!

With that in mind I am still going to talk to you about the role of carbs and fats… right now!

Carbohydrates

Good old carbs! These guys get a bit of a tough time from the fitness world, mostly from those who get a proper hard on and love to shoot a big load over Keto. The reality is they are our primary energy source and actually an important macronutrient for how we feel and function.

There are two types of carbohydrates, complex and non-complex. In truth this isn't all that relevant, one is a little more slow release and satiating, one is a little more sugary and more quick release, the best way to explain it is porridge is a complex carb and is therefore slow release and more satiating, 100g of porridge will have you feeling nice and full. Whereas Haribo is a non-complex carb and therefore quick release and such less satiating. 100g of sweets will not fill you up but could give you a nice quick release of energy if needed! It's why long-distance runners often carry jelly beans!

Neither are *'better'* or *'worse'* they just perform slightly different functions and therefore can carry different impacts on the body

The funny thing is if you listen to the Keto world, they demonise all carbs stating that they can spike insulin which causes fat gain. Firstly no, insulin spikes when eating carbs is what the body is meant to do, insulin allows the transportation of glucose to the blood and around the body. But also, the complex carbs are much slower release meaning the glucose is released slower into the body preventing rapid insulin spikes and yet this gets totally overlooked by our keto loving zealots.

I digress, ultimately carbs are a vital energy source, our body has two main energy sources. Carbs and Fats. Carbs are great for our explosive activity where we need rapid release of energy for performance.

Another good factor to carbs is, much like protein they're only 4kcal per gram, this allows you to consume good amounts without impacting heavily on your calorie intake. Particularly if you go down the route of fruit and veg that are cabs in make-up and very low calorie meaning you can eat high quantities for low calories. Not to mention they're packed full of vitamins and minerals.

From a sports perspective, if you're a professional athlete who trains at a high level for 4-5 hours a day, carbs are going to be really important for performance and recovery. However, if that isn't you then they're less important to 'prioritise' in fact the amount you consume should be down to your own personal preference.

A good rule of thumb would be, if you want to monitor all macros, calculate your calories, work out your protein and then you will know how many calories you have left for fats and carbs. I recommend trying to keep fats between 20-25% of your intake tops, I'll explain more about why shortly. Once you know how much Protein and fats you're aiming for, what's left can come from carbs.

Equally you can just eat the food you like, get the right protein and not worry about how much carbs and fats so long as you're within calories.

This is something so often overlooked in many aspects of 'getting in shape' is prioritising your own enjoyment in the process. I will talk about this from a training standpoint later but our food too has to include what we enjoy or we will find adherence, or chances of adhering long enough for lasting results will diminish.

Thanks to the emergence of some of, in my opinion, the shittest fad diets carbs are currently public enemy number one.
Our bodies primary, and preferred, energy source is being made out to be a bad thing and a key contributor to fat gain and a significant inhibitor to fat loss.
This just simply isn't true and the science doesn't support claims about carbs being in anyway bad for us.

However, there is this agenda within certain corners of the fitness world that will have you believe they are the devil.
One of the key arguments given is, as mentioned above, the spike in insulin levels caused when eating carbs.

Now, there is obviously a link between increased insulin levels and insulin resistance, and the knock-on link between obesity and insulin resistance therefore leading to type two diabetes and ultimately the link between obesity and type two diabetes. However, correlation and causation are not the same thing. Whilst carbs spike insulin levels this is not the same as requiring more insulin than your body can produce due to the overconsumption of calories causing insulin resistance.

When calories are controlled in line with what the body needs, the consumption of carbs, and subsequent insulin production, is normal.
The issue comes when the body is being fed more calories than it needs and we gain weight leading to a situation where to body can't keep up.

Simply having carbs resulting in a spike in insulin won't cause insulin resistance. Think about it this way, at every fatal car crash is an ambulance. This doesn't mean ambulances are killing people it also doesn't mean if you have a crash and they send an ambulance that you will die.

So just because those who are obese often end up becoming insulin resistance due to having to produce so much to keep up with their over consuming of calories, this doesn't mean insulin is causing people to gain weight or preventing them losing it.

Insulin is a vital chemical produced by the body and a totally normal response to eating carbs and shouldn't be used as fear mongering propaganda by zealot cunts trying to force their eating habits and worse still products or services onto you. Particularly when their 'methods' are essentially just glorified eating disorders positioned as 'essential for health'.

In short, some of the very best tasting foods are carbs and whilst some carbs act slightly differently to others in how their energy is released into the body, they are essentially only 4kcal per gram and fucking delicious so should absolutely be included and enjoyed as part of your daily eating, if you enjoy eating them.

The only caveat to this is those who are epileptic, in that instance only, would I recommend going low carb. This is because there is a significant link between the reduction in frequency and severity of seizures when carbs are reduced.

So, if you're wondering if you should eat carbs or not, I have created a nice flow diagram to help you decide.

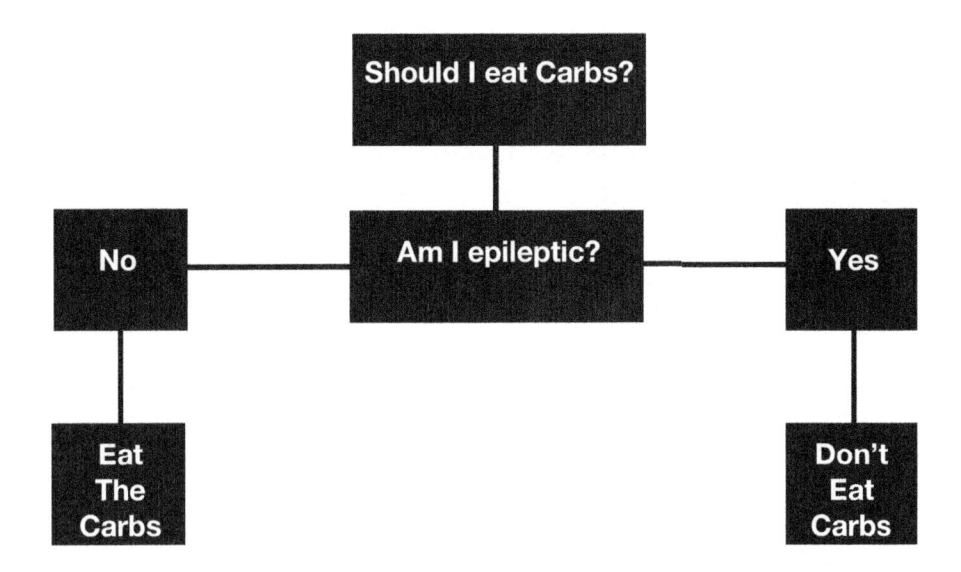

```
         Should I eat Carbs?
                  |
          Am I epileptic?
         /                \
       No                 Yes
        |                   |
   Eat The Carbs      Don't Eat Carbs
```

There may be some other instances where you may want to reduce or avoid carbs, this would come down to any intolerance or allergies. Obviously if eating them will make you very unwell I would avoid them. Also, if they have gone off and will also make you unwell, definitely avoid them then as well. Lastly if you don't like a certain carbohydrate... don't fucking eat it either.

But if you're not allergic or intolerant, they are well in date and you like them... eat away, just ensure it falls in line with what your body needs from a calorie standpoint.

My last point when it comes to carbs is a simple one. If someone is telling you to avoid them, they're bad for you, cause fat gain, are stored as fat if not burned off or that they cause an insulin spike that causes fat gain blah blah fucking blah... that person is almost certainly a cunt with zero joy in their life, probably orders sparkling water at a bar on a night out as a 'treat' and is almost certainly a virgin. Oh, and they're a lying cunt too.

So, that's carbs, what about fats? -

Fats.

When it comes to dietary fats these have had their time in the bad books as well over the years.
There was a time where people thought if you don't eat fat, you can't get fat.
Then there was the demonisation of some fats... saturated fats, oh they're evil fuckers, right?
Then we had a fats renaissance where going high fat high protein was the key to fat loss and even some fats got labelled as healthy fats!

So, what is the deal with fats? Well firstly they're the most calorific of all the macronutrients at a whopping 9kcal per gram. So, whilst you can eat over twice the food quantity of carbs and protein for the same amount of calories, this doesn't mean fats are something to fear or avoid either.

Quite the opposite, a 'healthy' diet is one that has balance and includes as much variety as possible and provides our body with what it needs from both a micro and macronutrient perspective. This includes fats.

Much like carbs the split of saturated and unsaturated fats will bring differing impacts on the body. Unsaturated fats tend to carry more nutritional value, more vitamins and minerals in the food that contains them, whereas saturated fats tend to offer much less nutritional value, but can offer something else... flavour!

As mentioned above a good rule of thumb for fat intake is somewhere between 20-25% of your calories from fats, ideally limiting saturated fats in this where possible. This is so that the body can get a good amount of vital vitamins and minerals that can only be found in fats whilst also not using up too many of your calories from fats alone.

Fats are the least satiating food so we will burn very few calories digesting them, also meaning that we can over consume them quite easily and if you want be able to get enough food quantity into your diet to keep you feeling well satiated, not to mention be able to get enough variety into your food, keeping fats to around 20-25% is going to help with this, a lot.

Now, some folk, the low carb folk, will have you believe that high fat means you burn more fat.
This is actually true, but we burn carbs and fat for energy, this is not the same as fat loss and should not be confused with fat loss.

If you have two fires next to each other, one burning coal and one burning logs they will each burn more of their chosen fuel than the other, respectively. It doesn't mean one is better than the other it just means it is burning more of what is being used as fuel.
Fat loss isn't about burning the fat we eat as energy it is about burning the stored fat that we have accumulated due to over consuming calories for so long. We can burn fat without losing fat, I.e., eating a high fat diet, doing lots of low intensity exercise but eating more calories than we burn will ultimately mean we burn a lot of 'fat' whilst actually gaining body fat. I will cover more of this later in the book.

There is one scenario that utilising fats can be really helpful. If you're trying to bring calories up, into a surplus, and you're struggling to reach your calorie target. Utilising fats more can hope boost calories up without having to increase food volume too much.

A handful of nuts, a spoon of peanut butter, half an avocado, a drizzle of oil can each add 200+ calories in the blink of an eye without feeling like you actually ate anything more than normal.

This is great when trying to increase calories but can be a significant player for why people think they're eating healthy and are in a deficit but may not actually be in a deficit and therefore not actually losing fat.

Despite this, fats are not something to be avoided, they're also not something you need to eat in large quantities to lose fat. In fact, as with both fats and carbs, as I already have said, the key is to eat the food you enjoy whilst staying within your calories and getting the right amount of protein consistently.

The more you overcomplicate it the less likely you are to eat what you enjoy and stay within calories and the more confused you will become, usually prompting you to think "fuck this" and just go back to old eating habits that caused the fat gain in the first place.

So, that's macronutrients, the nutrients we need in large quantities, but what about the ones we need in smaller amounts, the micronutrients? Let's have a proper look at these!

Micronutrients.

Whilst macros are needed in large quantities and fall into three simple groups micronutrients are required in much smaller amounts, fit into two groups, vitamins and minerals, of which there are an awful lot of each that make up each group, each playing a role in how our body functions and how we feel.

There are many vitamins and minerals that are pretty important to how we feel, vitamin C is really important to general health, especially when it comes to fighting off illnesses like the cold or flu. Vitamin D is a huge one, along with Iron, for our energy levels and our mood, in fact vitamin D from sunlight is one of the key components to regulating our mindset and a lack of vitamin D from sunlight in particular can leave us feeling really shit.

Another key mineral that helps our bodies to perform is fibre! Fibre helps our digestion, a lot, which if you're eating a high protein diet is going to be very important. A high protein diet can leave you pretty bunged up if fibre is low, so to avoid bloating, discomfort from a digestive perspective, as well as helping to stay regular from a bowel movement standpoint, get a good amount of fibre in your diet, you will thank yourself for it.
A good rule of thumb is between 20-30g of fibre per day, some may want a little more but it depends on how much protein you're eating etc.
In addition to this fibre actually comes in at a tiny 2kcal per gram meaning increasing that fibre intake won't hammer the calorie intake either. In fact, a good protein and fibre intake will work wonders for your satiety.

Now, when it comes to fibre, there are some folk out there that will have you believe that eating fibre or drinking a fibre drink before you eat will mean you can eat whatever you like and calories don't matter because it creates a barrier that stops the glucose entering the bloodstream and prevents insulin spikes. I will cover more on insulin later on but let's be clear. That is bollocks. Simply drinking a fibre drink, or changing the order you eat your food in to eat the fibre first won't allow you to eat whatever you like.

Fibre is helpful and should be kept within the recommended range but it isn't magic and certainly won't enable you to eat whatever you like.

Now for me to sit and list all the vitamins and minerals, what they do to your body, how much you need etc. would take fucking ages and the purpose of this book is to make your life easier not overload with information that when you break it all down, isn't that relevant so here is my top advice on vitamins and minerals.

Aim to get as much variety into your diet as you can, plenty of fruit and vegetables, a good mix of fat sources, like nuts and seeds and ensure you get a good amount of fibre and natural sunlight.

If you can do that you will be fine, if however, like many, you struggle to get enough variety into your diet due to food preferences and dietary behaviours then when it comes to vitamins and minerals you can either supplement the specific ones you feel you're missing or used a good quality multi-vitamin to ensure your body is getting what it needs, that you might be missing due to the food you're eating.

There is little need to make it more complicated than that, because let's face it, you could easily end up spending a small fortune to supplement so many things that in the grand scheme of things may not make any noticeable difference to how you feel and function.

Which brings me nicely onto the next topic which is supplements.

Supplements.

The supplement industry is fucking massive nowadays and extends far beyond what it used be.
But there is a lot of benefit to sticking to the basics, a steady old Berocca and a chewable multi-vit!

But supplements these days aren't just about topping up your vitamins and minerals, in fact you could easily split them into two categories, Performance based supplements and general health and well-being supplements.

Both are 90% hot air designed to lure you in and take your money but on both sides of the divide there are some really useful supplements that might just be worth incorporating into your daily lifestyle and I will cover them off for you now.

When it comes to vitamins and minerals my best recommendation is this;

A daily Vitamin C, like Berocca is definitely a good start, it'll help you keep those common colds at bay!
A daily multi-vitamin will also ensure there's a good mix of all the essentials you need for optimum health and how your body functions.
Then we have fibre!! If you can't eat enough from what you eat daily a good fibre supplement could absolutely help.
Vitamin D, this one…is best from sunlight but if you live in the UK you may struggle, so short of sunbeds each week a vitamin d supplement will suffice.

You could prioritise gut health by adding a pre and/or probiotic but this isn't essential, especially if you have good variety to your duet and a decent fibre intake.

Besides that, you should be just fine from a vitamin and mineral perspective, as with everything it is always best to keep it as simple as possible otherwise, you'll be spending a fucking fortune on supplements, most of which you don't really need.

When it comes to performance-based supplements this is even more confusing and there are so many supplements positioned as essential that in reality are just a complete waste of money.

The role of any supplement, be it training based or nutrient based is to supplement what you already get, rather like financial supplements, they top up to bridge the gap between what you have and need.

Performance wise the only two supplements I genuinely believe are worth their salt are;

A good quality whey protein isolate, or plant-based alternative, and creatine monohydrate.

A good quality whey is always useful as it enables you to get more protein in, if it is an isolate, it'll be higher protein and lower calorie bringing more variety to how you get your protein in without smashing your calories. It's not a 'requirement' to use protein powder but most people struggle getting enough protein in throughout the day and a decent quality protein powder is the perfect way to address this. Especially as it is way more acceptable to drink a quick shake than to walk around with a chicken breast!

A good rule of thumb is to aim for around 20-30g per scoop/serving and somewhere around the 60-120kcal per serving mark. Plant based protein powders can tend to be a little higher in calories but there are still some very good, lower calorie options out there!

There are some circumstances where a higher calorie protein shake might be of benefit, again when trying to up calories into a surplus, a higher calorie (and therefore higher protein) powder can both up protein and calories without the need to increase actual food intake but in my opinion, there is still little to no need for the 900kcal+ Mass Gainer shakes, especially given adding mass isn't just about lifting heaving and smashing a 1000kcal protein shake.

Then we have creatine monohydrate. This is probably the most researched, tested and studied supplement out there. The information on how it works is plentiful and it is one of the safest supplements on the market.
Its job is to help produce more creatine which in turn helps the body hold more water, glycogen, in the muscles which helps us perform more explosively, gives a fuller look to our muscles and provides a little more energy for training and repair/recovery.

There are a few different ways to introduce creatine to your diet, some favour a loading phase followed by a tapering phase where you double the dose for a couple of weeks then back off and then have a couple of weeks break before starting again.

When you look at the evidence in the meta-analysis of creatine consumption vs impact on performance and aesthetics there is no additional benefit to this when compared to having the standard serving daily for the duration of your training life.

In my opinion it is best to just have the recommended serving each day than to worry about trying to saturate your body then tapering back.

That being said, creatine is a valuable addition for both fat loss and muscle building goals due to the improvements in training performance and how it helps you look from an aesthetic perspective too.

Outside of those two... the rest is basically hot air!

BCAA's, EAA's, CLA's, pre workout, intraworkout and all in-between are there for one reason and one reason alone... to take your fucking money!
Now, if you find that you perform better with a pre workout or recover better with BCAA's and the placebo effect is worth the expense, then have at it but from the research studies out there the impact you will get from all these products is minimal at best.

If you're competing in a physique competition then you might be keen to use Performance Enhancing Drugs (PEDs or gear) or to use fat strippers and a cocktail of supplements and in this instance the fraction of a percentage difference could be the difference between winning and not even placing so in that arena it may make sense to spend a fortune on supplements and PEDs etc. as you're literally competing. But for all of us who aren't competing and are just looking to get in better shape the suggested potential and very minimal benefits will not outweigh the cost and therefore mean it is just not worth spending money on this stuff.

In fact, here are some of my thoughts and recommendations around the most commonly bought products;

BCAA's & EAA's - amino acids are found in protein, if you're eating enough protein and using protein powder you will be getting all the amino acids, both branch-chain and essential so supplementing them will be less than fucking pointless.

CLA's or fat strippers - these just raise your core body temperature and are often packed with copious amounts of caffeine. Just drink a coffee if needs be or have a can or Monster as in reality, they might help you burn 10 calories and for £50 a bottle that's a terrible return.

Pre-workout - this is the biggest con on the market for me. Have a black coffee or a monster before you train, better still eat some carbs about an hour before you train and have a strong coffee and you'll be just fine. You don't need to be ripping your own skin off and twitching like a kid with Tourette's for a good workout!
Now most pre-workout drinks are essentially just high caffeine drinks, as are a number of the fat burners and strippers already mentioned. So, what about caffeine itself?
Caffeine could potentially be viewed as a performance supplement and whilst there are some people who will try to claim coffee and caffeine are at a detriment to fat loss goals this is actually not true.
Caffeine will do a couple of things that actually can be very useful for fat loss. Firstly, it can raise your core body temperature, this slight elevation of your body temp will actually mean you burn ever so slightly more calories at rest. Another significant factor is that it will actually mean you jitter and move a little more, again raising you resting calorie expenditure. It is why almost all physique competitors utilise caffeine supplements as well as drinking black coffee. There is then the final potential benefit of including caffeine,

especially through drinking coffee. It can actually help to suppress appetite slightly, something that will make being in a calorie deficit a little easier to navigate. When you look at it this way, adding caffeine, either through black coffee or caffeine supplements can be a very useful tool to slightly accelerate results.

Intra-workout drinks - unless you're training for over 90 mins or doing endurance training like marathons… you don't need intra workout drinks like isotonics. They're just expensive and high calorie and you won't be depleting glycogen and electrolytes enough to need to replenish them.
Something to consider here is, if you are training over 90 minutes and want a good rehydration drink for replenishing electrolytes, sodium and sugars is ensure you opt for a drink that will actually deliver that.
Prime is a very popular 'rehydration drink' but when you look at the quantities of electrolytes vs both the recommended/required servings and other drinks such as Powerade you'd realise Prime is not only obscenely expensive but also offers very little by way of minerals to actually aid rehydration and the replenishment of electrolytes. So be mindful not to buy based off of 'marketing' and to actually look at the quality of the product you're about to consume.

Then we have L-Carnitine. In reality this has been around for fucking years but in recent years has risen to the top of the fat loss supplement tree and you guessed it… it's fucking pointless. L-Carnitine will help the conversion of fat into energy. It can therefore boost in gym performance and help you 'burn more fat'. However, as already discussed, burning more fat and losing fat are two entirely independent things not to be confused. A bit like identical twins, they may appear the same but I can assure you, they're two totally different entities.

So, do you need it? Much like all the other supplements, if you find it helps then great but whatever you do, don't spend money on it thinking it will be the magic bullet for fat loss, because in short... It fucking won't be.

In almost all cases of performance supplements you can get everything you need without spending a fortune.

Another thing that gets a lot of attention when it doesn't really need it is our nutrient timing which is what we will look at now.

Nutrient timing.

I am sure you have all heard a statement around nutrient or meal timing before be that; 'don't eat carbs after 6pm',' breakfast is the most important meal of the day' or 'you need 30g protein within 30mins of training'.

When it comes to nutrient timing there is a lot of information out there and almost all of it is what I would call utter bollocks.

Now, from a sports nutrition perspective, when dealing with athletes of various disciplines there are a lot of benefits to getting your meals in at certain times.

Eating 2-4hours before intense exercise will bring some significant benefits to performance, which if you're a performance athlete is going to be of benefit to your success. Much like eating a good amount of carbs and protein within a 45minute window of training will bring a fractional percentage increase of recovery and therefore aid future performance. Which can only be a good thing for a performance athlete whose income is dependent on success.

But, unless you are a performance athlete or a physique competitor where success, in terms of beating other people, is fundamental to your life, nutrient timing is far less important than you might think.

In fact, eating in line with your lifestyle and preferences is way more important.

I'll break it down into three sections;

Eating before training
Eating after training
Meal timings

When it comes to eating before you train, whilst some people feel they *'need'* to eat before they train to perform at their best other people find eating before a session actually hinders them as it makes them feel sick and therefore focus less on their training.
I would always say when it comes to eating before you train it is down to two things, your own preference but also the time of day you're training.
If you're training first thing in the morning, I expect you might struggle to eat beforehand and not feel like shit. You may be able to and that's great but many wont so potentially not eating before training would be of benefit. Not to fat loss, as some cunts would suggest *cough, fasted cardio wankers, cough* but just because you won't feel like you're about to chunder at the end of each set.

On the flip side, if you're training later in the day, you may find eating a couple of hours before is necessary to give you enough energy after a long day to smash your session.
In short it is largely down to what you feel is best for you. The reported benefits of eating within a window of time before a session will bring such minimal impact just do what feels best for you.

When it comes to eating after training, especially the 30g of protein within a 45minute window... let's be honest, again this can yield a fractional percentage improvement for MPS in terms of that protein going direct to the muscles but if you're getting enough protein in throughout the day it really doesn't matter if you eat protein right after you train.
Some people find they're hungrier after they train and again, I would say if you feel you need to eat post workout then have at it. For other people they just aren't hungry straight after a session and therefore trying to eat can make them feel like they're force feeding themselves. So, my advice here is somewhat the same as eating before a session. Do whatever the fuck works best for you.

As for meal timings in general some folk will say breakfast is the most important meal of the day, others say don't eat breakfast it makes you fat, other people then say not eating breakfast puts you into starvation mode which we know now doesn't exist. Other people claim if you eat carbs after 6pm they make you fat or if you eat too late you can't burn it off and it gets stored as fat... so what's the truth?

The truth is this... eat when you fucking want to.
If you can't think of anything worse than not having breakfast, have breakfast!
Equally if you aren't fussed, skipping breakfast could be a useful tool to being in a deficit, more on this later!

As for eating late in the day, it doesn't matter. A calorie is a unit of measurement, it doesn't double in value after a certain time and equally if you don't 'burn it off' straight away it isn't stored as fat.
We store calories as fat when we consistently eat too many of the cunts. It has nothing to do with the time of day we eat them.

Equally, what is worth addressing is the underlying relationship with food, boredom eating, comfort eating etc. Because most people aren't smashing a tub of Ben and Jerry's for breakfast and eating late at night can be a contributing factor to going over calories. But it isn't the eating late doing it, it's the extra calories so managing your overall intake is key here.

Some people find by pushing their first meal of the day back later in the day that it is easier to factor in some of the nicer things in the evening or that they simply aren't as hungry so snack less.

Others will find that eating more much earlier in the day leaves them feeling fuller so they snack less. The key thing here is finding what works best for you as everyone is different, and whilst there are techniques that may help or be useful there is no hard and fast, one size fits all way to manage your calories and include the food you love.

So much so that as long as you manage your daily intake, along with protein intake, and are consistent with it, eating the food you like in a way that works for you, you will be more than fine. The time of those meals throughout the day and in relation to your training doesn't really matter.

What you may find is with calories and protein it is easier and more forgiving on your body and better for performance to get your calories and protein in from regular meals at regular intervals than to try and smash it all from just one meal per day.

Something that can undoubtedly help you on this journey is monitoring your calorie intake to ensure you're getting the right amount for your goal. But before we get balls deep into that, one thing that is massively overlooked by almost everyone is the importance of hydration.

Hydration.

Easily one of the most overlooked elements of optimum nutrition is hydration.
Staying well hydrated is so much more than just drinking 2L per day.
Hydration itself plays a significant role in how our body functions, recovers and how our brain functions too.
Which is why it is so important to strive for good hydration each day.
Our hydration plays a massive role in regulating our core body temperature, keeping our joints lubricated, organs functioning properly, preventing infections as well as transporting nutrients to cells.

Everything about how our bodies works requires good hydration and so many areas of our life are affected if we're dehydrated.

The fact is most people think dehydration just means your piss turns yellow and being well hydrated means pissing all the time and it being clear.

It is a lot more than that.

In fact, proper hydration improves our brain clarity and cognitive function, so you not only pee clearer you think clearer too! When we think clearer with better brain function and clarity everything runs much smoother in general!
Not to mention you will experience a better mood, feel more awake and have more energy!

Then we have the fact that your body recovers and your muscles function better when adequately hydrated.
Being dehydrated will lead to cramping muscles, stiffness, delayed recovery and a greater risk of injury. It also has a

knock-on effect on your sleep too because if your muscles can't actually relax properly due to poor hydration your brain won't shut off as effectively when trying to sleep leaving you feeling restless and unable to sleep properly. And let's face it, no one is pleasant to be around and able to function properly when we're tired as fuck!

Drinking enough throughout the day doesn't just help us with how well our brain works, how well we sleep and how well our muscles recover. It also plays a vital role in ridding the body of toxins, something that is vital for our general health. It's why if you don't drink enough, you can get a UTI as your body can't get rid of the toxins effectively leading to infections.

So, if being well hydrated is going to aid recovery, sleep, mood, brain function and ensure our body is functioning at its best how much water do we need each day and does it just need to be water we take on?

A general rule of thumb is to drink between 2-3litres per day but it doesn't have to be from plain water.
In fact, hydration comes from almost everything we drink and some of what we eat.
Fruit and vegetables are often high in water meaning they play a key and understated role in aiding our hydration.
Water is obviously the best source for hydration but we can also get hydration from fruit juices, carbonated drinks as well as teas and coffees. It is worth noting that tea and coffee are diuretics, so whilst they will hydrate us, they will cause us to go to the toilet more frequently so it is advised not to solely rely on coffee or tea to hydrate you.

In fact, almost everything you drink will hydrate you with the exception of alcohol which actually dehydrates you.

But knowing that you don't have to just drink plain water can be a significant plus when trying to hit that intake. Especially when you consider it wasn't uncommon for PTs to claim drinking squash or cordial didn't count. Fucking shitcunts at it again with their bullshit misinformation.

What his worth highlighting, in the pursuit of optimum hydration is that you could lose up to, or more than, a litre of water during a workout, 80% of which needs to be replenished in order to replace any loss electrolytes.

However, the need to drink isotonic drinks during workouts is only really required if you are exercising for longer than 90 minutes because when you train beyond 90 minutes you will be depleting your body of stored glycogen and electrolytes. If you're training less than that you really don't need isotonic or electrolyte drinks.

In fact, the best intra-workout drinks for anyone training under 90 minutes is either water or squash.
The trouble is there are a number of products on the market that position themselves as 'essential' for consuming before, during or after a workout and almost everyone has no need for them. But there was more on this when I covered off supplements.

In short, you really want to prioritise your hydration throughout the day in order to perform and recover to your absolute best. It really does govern so much of how our bodies operate and how we feel in general.
It doesn't have to just be from plain water but you do want to try and be drinking between 2-3 litres per day.

What about drinking more than 3 litres of water?

Well, too much of anything will be bad and too much water will drown you. But let's be honest you would have to drink a lot to cause you real issues.

If you're very active, training every day of the week you will probably be drinking much more than 2-3 litres and that is fine. For many people a good start point is 2litres and to build on that over time.

There is an added benefit to increasing your water intake, you will be up and down to the loo more often which will increase your step count and ensure you don't have time for other people's bullshit!

You will also notice your body holds onto less water the more you drink which can aid with digestion and bloating so it really does pay to keep that fluid intake high.

I promise you, if you bring your intake up you will notice the benefits very quickly.

Now that we have covered one of the most underrated factors for improving health and how we feel let's get stuck into the thick of it by looking at how best to manage your calorie intake.

Tracking Calories.

Tracking calories is a tool to aid fat loss. It isn't a requirement by any means and may not be the best tool for everyone but I am a firm believer of *'What gets measured, gets improved'*.

Think about it this way, if you know you need to eat a certain amount of calories each day the best way to ensure you're doing that is to keep a track of just how many calories you're eating each day to make sure you're actually in line with what your body needs.

I guarantee if you wanted to save money, let's say for a deposit on a house, you'd pay pretty close attention to what's going out of your account vs what's coming in each month. You might have a little spreadsheet, do regular checks, spending caps, limit social events and in no time, you'll be a cracking little saver. No one would call you obsessive or suggest that is in anyway detrimental to your life. In fact, it is often highly encouraged you monitor your finances!

However, if you apply the same principle to your diet, because after all fat loss is simply the result of consistently eating less than you burn people are awfully quick to suggest you're obsessive or it's not good for you.

Now, some people may find it a bit much, and this I fully understand, the industry has been a festering turd of an industry and created more diets that promote disordered eating or even drive people to eating disorders than I care to admit.
So, for some, being conscious of their intake could be a trigger. That being said it doesn't distract from the fact that

the requirement for fat loss is a deficit and the best way to ensure you're in one is to know what you're eating.

So, for the 90% of people who aren't suffering from eating disorders tracking is a very useful tool.
Not least because it gives you a clear picture of how you're doing but it also allows you to learn how many calories are in certain foods which can allow you to become more intuitive in your approach.

Tracking is more of a short-term behaviour that generates knowledge and allows for a more flexible approach in the long term.
If we find over time things are slowing or going backwards you probably pay a little more attention to what you're eating to reign it in a little. Other times we eat a little more intuitively and worry slightly less.

When it comes to tracking itself there are some things you can do to make your life way easier.
There are a number of calorie tracker apps out there. My personal favourite is MyFitnessPal, it's what I use personally and encourage my clients to use as well. It's incredibly comprehensive and has just about every single food ever needed in it. That being said there are a few other alternatives out there too, NutraCheck being one of them.

When using an app like MyFitnessPal, don't use the app to tell you how many calories you should be eating. This is because it will ask you about how much weight you want to lose each week and us humans always pick the most available. This means you get given fuck all calories as a target and will find it really hard to stick to. So instead use a calorie calculator, like my free one for example www.redefineacademy.com/calorie-calculator to calculate them for you as this will take into account your activity level and give you a much more sustainable target.

Also don't track your activity in MyFitnessPal (MFP) because each calorie you burn it will tell you, you can eat it again, which if you have calculated calories properly and included activity in working out your deficit, will already be included in your target.

When it comes to tracking you will never be 100% accurate but weighing food out as you make it will always help improve the accuracy. However, try to not fall for the trap of *'making it look good on paper'* and instead try to be as accurate as possible. It's no good MFP saying you only had 300kcal for breakfast if it was actually 500kcal as you will eat like it was only 300kcal for the rest of the day and could potentially end up going over without realising.

A lack of accuracy is one of the biggest reasons why people who think they're in a deficit actually aren't in one.

Then there is how you monitor things; your success isn't determined by what you do each day in isolation. It is about what you do consistently over an extended period of time. One high calorie meal or high calorie day won't instantly make you fat just the same as eating one low calorie salad or having a low calorie day doesn't instantly make you lose fat.

Instead of looking day to day and trying to constantly recover and adjust day to day based on the previous day, monitor your calories over a 7 day period and just try to average the right calories over that period.

If you're averaging the right calories each week for an extended period of time you will be making great progress even if each week includes some higher calorie days. It takes the pressure off you to be perfect each day and means you can track calories, eat the right amount but still feel like you can enjoy your lifestyle a little more too.

Tracking calories won't guarantee results but it will make it far easier to get results and even easier to pinpoint elements of your lifestyle that might need addressing in order to reduce calorie intake in line with your goal.
After all you will be eating the food anyway, may as well track it to help make more informed decisions.

Something I am a believer in is when done correctly tracking helps us break the all or nothing mentality that the diet industry has conditioned us to have, so much so almost all fad diets set unrealistic expectations on us and that's something that I'm going to talk to you about a little later in this section.

Now, I am aware that some of you will be thinking *"But Paul, we don't all absorb the same amount of calories from the food we eat. Surely this means tracking is pointless?"*

Here's the thing, yes, we do all absorb different amounts of calories from the food we eat. But no one is metabolising MORE calories than is actually in the food you're eating. So, the very worst case scenario is if you track a food that has say 100kcal in it you absorb all 100kcal. The reality is that you may not even absorb that much meaning the likelihood is you're absorbing less than you're eating.

This doesn't mean tracking is pointless, quite the opposite actually. It means realistically you still want to ensure what goes in your mouth is in line with what your body needs. If you do that you will know you're never going to be eating too many, but you could be absorbing less than you think, which would be a bonus.

Before we get to that though, it's worth addressing something that we have all heard of and no doubt all have wildly different ideas about what this thing actually is and how it works.

I am talking, of course, about your metabolism.

Your Metabolism.

Let's face it we have all heard claims made by fitness influencers referring to your metabolism. Fuck, it's not just influencers making claims, I can guarantee Julie at work or Sharon down the pub has laid claim to something that has slowed, increased, boosted or broken their metabolism. So, what the actual fuck is your metabolism, what does it do, how do we *'control'* it, can we break it, fix or boost it?

In short, your metabolism is the fancy word for the **chemical processes required to sustain life.**
It is everything your body does to keep you alive.
Those chemical processes then require energy to be completed which is why our BMR stands for basal metabolic rate - the calories burned at rest to sustain life.

Your metabolic rate is governed by how well your body can function and complete the various chemical processes required to keep you alive each and every single day.

This fact highlights why anyone claiming that your metabolism may in fact be broken is chatting utter shit. Because if you broke your metabolism, I.e., your body can't complete the chemical processes required to sustain life… you would be dead.

So, we can rule out a broken metabolism ever being the cause for failing to lose fat, because 100% of people with a *'broken'* metabolism… i.e., the dead… don't struggle to lose fat. Because they're dead!

How about a slow metabolism or food that boosts your metabolism, is there any truth to that?

Well not really, but also potentially. Basically, it's not a straight forward yes or no.

Most of the *'superfoods'* that people claim *'boost your metabolism'* will do fuck all. They're often low in calories and have many nutrients to them but in terms of boosting your metabolism, i.e., increasing the calories you burn at rest, they will do next to fuck all.
In fact, if you want to explore food that helps you burn more calories at rest, you're essentially looking at protein.
Outside of that almost all food you eat will do very little for *'boosting'* your metabolism. However, everything and I mean everything you eat will trigger various chemical processes and hormone productions. It is how your body is designed to work, so you could argue that all foods *'boost'* or *'kickstart'* your metabolism given they require a release of calories to digest and absorb the nutrients.
This is probably why people constantly get their dicks hard over ginger or cinnamon and other spices because they want to position their pseudoscience bullshit as being *'metabolically beneficial'* when in reality anything you eat will trigger your body to burn calories aka… *'boosting'* or *'speeding'* up your metabolism.

So, if in reality the concept of boosting or speeding up your metabolism is just increasing the calories burned at rest and is triggered by literally anything you eat meaning it's basically an industry con to lure you in. What about a slow metabolism? Is that real?

There are conditions that will reduce the amount of calories you burn at rest. So yes, a *'slower metabolism'* is kind of true, just like some people appear to have a *'faster metabolism'*.

What you often find is the slower metabolism group are much less active in general than those we perceive to have a fast metabolism meaning they simply burn less calories than their more active counterparts creating the illusion of a slow or fast metabolism.

But when you consider your metabolic rate is dictated by what you burn at rest and not through activity there are very few conditions where it would actually lower the calories you burn at rest however here are some factors that can reduce what you burn at rest;

Age - as we get older, we burn less calories at rest, this is largely due to sarcopenia (muscle loss with ageing) and as we know the more muscle you have the more calories you burn at rest.

Gaining body fat - the more fat your body holds the less calories you will burn at rest. This is more than likely due to having a lower activity level but holding more body fat will mean less calories will be burned at rest.

A lack of muscle mass - the more muscle you hold the more calories you burn at rest so if you're losing muscle, through sarcopenia or just hold very little muscle in general you will burn less calories at rest.

Hormonal issues such as;
Hypothyroidism, PCOS and menopause all significant reduce the amount of calories we burn at rest. Menopause also can accelerate sarcopenia as well adding fuel to the fire so to speak. There's more on this later in the book.

In all these instances, however, it does not mean you can't lose fat. It simply means that you may need to work slightly harder, adhere to a slightly larger deficit or be a little more patient with how fast results are achieved.

The big thing to remember is that even if you have a condition that reduces your BMR, it won't suddenly mean you're an exception to science and are therefore no longer governed by thermodynamics.

The fact still remains in order to drop body fat you need to eat less calories than you burn, it just means you may potentially have a lower BMR than you used to which means your TDEE is lower than you perhaps realise.

Now, if you focus on resistance training, managing calories, a good step count and getting a good amount of protein you can begin to increase the amount of calories you burn at rest and therefore create the illusion of *'speeding up'* your metabolism.

Anyone claiming you need to manage hormone levels or buy a plan based on your body type or to *'fix your metabolism'* are basically chatting shit in order to sell their one size fits all plan at your expense.

But what about those people who claim that our metabolism, and our body in general, has a preferred weight?
That even if we diet down our body will always return to its 'preferred weight'?
Well, mi amigos, we call them lying shitcunts and luckily for you, I am going to tell you why.

Set Point Theory.

So, what about Set Point Theory?

Set Point Theory is just that, a theory, so not a fact, that our bodies have an ideal weight it likes to sit at and that no matter how hard we diet, once we stop, we will rebound back up to that *'ideal weight'*.

Sound familiar? It's the modern day equivalent to Somatotypes. Another theory claiming our body type or weight is predetermined.

Here's the thing, anyone who has lost weight and regained it will relate to set point theory, and given about 90% of people regain the weight lost… AND MORE (remember that) within 12 months of losing it, it is not hard to see why people would buy into the theory that their body has a *'set point'* it likes to sit at.

The trouble is set point theory suggests we have a weight we would *'sit at'* naturally but there are two things that immediately discredit that without even needing the science to do any heavy lifting.
The first thing is the millions of people who have lost weight and maintained it for years. They immediately discredit the theory as they are proof that you can maintain results long term and not rebound.

Then we have the majority of people who do rebound and regain the weight back after losing who go onto gain even more weight.

For set point theory to be correct it would mean people would naturally lose weight too after gaining it to sit at their *'natural'* weight.

But we don't see people gaining fat for a while then miraculously dropping it without even trying. In fact, when the weight is increasing there is seemingly no limit to how much it can gain by. Something that clearly contradicts the claims of set point theory.

The reason why most people regain the weight they lose within 12 months is not because their body is hardwired to sit at a certain weight.
It is because the approach taken to lose weight wasn't a long term approach and taught them nothing about maintaining their progress.

If you drastically change your diet and lifestyle for a few months and lose weight and the minute you are happy with the results stop doing what was working in order to return to your *'normal'* eating habits and activity level. It isn't set point theory that's at play. It's that your *'normal'* eating habits and activity level are not aligned. Your normal behaviours have you eating more calories than you burn.

It isn't that you're happier at a certain weight, it's purely that you're just used to eating too many calories and when you try to lose weight adopt a short term approach you could never stick to. So, there is absolutely no wonder or surprise you rebound, and some.

The way to tackle it is through adopting a long term lifestyle approach that you can enjoy and requires less disruption to your current habits.
That way you're more likely to enjoy it, feel like you're not on a diet and you will make it much easier to maintain as well.

Its why people yo-yo with fad diets, because you'll never do it or longer than a couple of months at best and then it's back to you *'old ways'*. The very same ways that caused the fat gain to begin with.

So, whilst it's a lovely thought that your weight regain is beyond your control and the universe determined long ago that you should be a fat cunt, I have bad news.
That isn't the case and this theory is another example of the industry doing all it can to rid you of any blame and feed you lies to keep you at arm's length from actually knowing how to get results and keep them.

The good news, however, is that with the right approach you can break free of the yo-yo dieting and finally get the results you dream of, and keep them! It just requires a longer term approach and avoiding all the bollocks the industry tells you.

This brings me rather nicely onto our next topic, that the industry loves to point the finger at both for why you might gain weight and how to lose weight.
All of which, have fuck all to do with fat gain and fat loss by the way.

I am talking about hormones, so let's take a look at what the industry tells us, how they work and what is actually important.

Hormones.

Something that is a hot topic in the fitness world, in part thanks to the emergence of the Keto diet and all the shitcunts who promote it, is that we need to manage certain hormone levels in order to lose body fat.
This, firstly, is simply not true because when calories are controlled in line with what the body needs and we are getting the right balance of nutrients our bodies themselves manage our hormone levels but in order to explain this I will explain in detail about hormones for you.

One hormone that gets way more limelight than any other is Insulin.

Insulin is a reactionary hormone, meaning it is produced in response to something happening in the body. That thing is eating food, namely carbohydrates.

The primary role of insulin is to transport glucose into the bloodstream so it can be transported around the body.
When we eat carbs, the body breaks them down and the sugars/ glucose is then transported into the bloodstream.

Now, there are people who are born Type 1 diabetic and as such their body doesn't produce insulin naturally so are insulin dependent. They also need to closely monitor the amount of sugars/ glucose in their blood to ensure their levels remain stable.

Something that gets a lot of hysteria in the fitness industry is insulin resistance caused by obesity.
There is a large amount of people, who get their dicks nice and hard over the Keto diet, who will have you believe obesity is result of high levels of insulin, leading to insulin resistance rather than recognising that actually high insulin levels leading

to insulin resistance is actually a symptom of obesity not a cause.

In order to explain this, I want you to picture your body is like the London Underground.
Passengers are calories and insulin is a conductor on the train to ensure a smooth and steady flow of passengers on and off the train at the right points.

If the amount of passengers increases, I.e., you eat more food (especially carbs) your body will increase the number of conductors for that period of time. In short, your body will produce more insulin to transport the glucose into the blood. This is perfectly normal and the job of insulin. If you're not having insulin 'spikes' when eating carbs, you're in big trouble.
Now, the issues arise when there is, consistently, too many *'people'* (calories) getting on 'the train' (your body) at any one time.

Your body will try to produce more insulin to cope but as you become overweight and obese your body will reach a point it simply can't keep up and so effectively downs tools and stops producing insulin. This is what Type 2 Diabetes or insulin resistance is.

In simple terms the conductor simply can't do its job of transporting *'people'* on and off at the right stops because too many people are getting on and they're simply overwhelmed.

Now, if you slow the flow of people onto the train over time (reduce your calories into a deficit) your body will begin to reverse pre diabetes and potentially even type 2 diabetes because as you lose fat and ultimately eat less calories your body is able to produce a level of insulin that can manage the flow of glucose effectively.

This is all relating to Lifestyle/ diet impacted insulin resistance. I am aware of other causes for diabetes but for those who are pre-diabetic or type 2 diabetic due to being overweight or obese, this is what has been going on.

In fact, type 2 diabetes only used to be seen in the majority of cases in adults, particularly those over a certain age as they aged and began to become less active, were burning less calories and ultimately gaining a bit of weight. As a result, in later life people began developing what was originally known as Adult-Onset Diabetes.
However, in more recent years more and more people have been developing Type 2 Diabetes and it has even been observed in children due to an increasingly more sedentary lifestyle and the ever increasing rise in obesity across all age groups.

The best and most effective way to reverse it and prevent it is to understand two things.
Type 2 Diabetes or Lifestyle induced insulin resistance is caused by becoming overweight or obese due to consuming too many calories on the regular, and not from eating carbs spiking insulin.
The second thing to understand is that to prevent or reverse it simply requires you to drop body fat by consuming less calories consistently. When you do this your body is able to produce the correct levels of insulin to manage the flow of glucose effectively.

Once you understand insulin is a reactionary hormone it is easy to understand that you don't need to manage insulin levels to achieve fat loss or prevent fat gain.
The correlation between obesity and insulin resistance is just that, a correlation and not a causation. In short, insulin isn't causing obesity, obesity is causing insulin resistance.

Much like at every fatal car crash there will be an ambulance, they're also at most non-fatal ones too. Now you could extrapolate that and claim ambulances are the cause of fatalities at car crashes because everyone who has died in one has had an ambulance present. But we know that isn't the case, it is a correlation not a causation. Insulin spikes or insulin resistance are to the obese what ambulances are to fatal car crashes, reactionary. They're there because of what happened, what happened wasn't caused because they were there.

Another bullshit claim the keto cunts will make is that keeping insulin levels low helps with satiety and prevents hunger. I have heard people genuinely claim that eating bread and drinking alcohol or fizzy drinks at the start of a meal makes you eat more.

Now, I don't know about you but when I was a kid and we went out for dinner my folks would have a hissy fit if I guzzled a coke and stuffed my face with bread before my main meal. I can still hear my folks now *"Don't fill up on that or you won't eat your main"*. And they were right, if you eat more food, even if it causes an insulin spike this won't cause you to want to eat more food.

This is because hunger and satiety aren't really controlled by insulin levels. They're caused by two entirely different hormones, Leptin and Ghrelin.

When we begin to feel hungry this is due to the production of Ghrelin in your stomach to signal to your brain, you're hungry and need to eat. Leptin on the other hand is what we produce in order to decrease hunger and increase satiety.

What is strange is that these two play a far more significant role in appetite and satiety than insulin, and poorly managing appetite and satiety could be a cause of overeating and over consuming calories. Yet these two hormones are never really discussed. Why is this? Because in short fat gain and fat loss isn't achieved by hormone management.

Your body produces hormones in response to what is happening in your body. Fat loss is caused not by hormone levels falling outside of a normal range of production it is caused by consistently eating too many calories.

Manage your calories effectively and guess what?! Your body manages the production of your hormone levels just fine!

Ways you can effectively manage your appetite include not waiting until you're starving hungry to eat *cough,* Fasting, *cough* if you delay eating until you're starving, you're likely to eat much quicker meaning you could end up eating more calories before your body can signal the brain to stop you eating.

Having a drink of water or a black coffee can reduce appetite a little when you do feel hungry which can help between meals.
Best of all though would be increasing your protein intake. Protein is the most satiating food meaning you will feel fuller for longer. Including plenty of protein in your diet will help manage satiety levels helping to prevent overeating. Including high protein snacks between meals can be the difference to feeling full most of the day so you don't overeat and ultimately poorly managing appetite and frequently over consuming calories.

As I said though, manage what you eat, how many calories and how much protein and your body will handle managing your hormones.

Now, I couldn't talk about hormones and the impact they have on your progress without discussing how hormones, and in particular the hormones associated with menstruation can impact fat loss for women.

If you're a guy, you're welcome to skip this next section, but ladies, this could be the most important section in the whole book for you.

Female Fat Loss.

Now, whilst everything I just explained is very much correct there is one thing to take into account when seeking fat loss and that is if you're biologically a woman.

If you are, then when it comes to your journey it will differ slightly from that of us males.

Firstly, we have the simple fact that due to the total amount of mass held by men and women comparatively, particularly muscle mass, men will burn on average 30% more calories than women. Meaning if you put a guy and a girl on the treadmill at the same settings and had them race to burn 100kcals the guy would get there a lot quicker.

If that wasn't unfair enough you then have the simple fact that affect of hormonal cycles between men and women is very different.

Throughout a 28 day cycle men's hormones stay fairly regular and constant, creating a more level playing field for fat loss. The same can't be said for the ladies.

Your monthly menstrual cycle will have very clear impacts on how you feel, perform and what you weigh at any given time of your period.

Now, I am acutely aware that as a 35 year old bloke (at time of writing) I have never and will never have a menstrual cycle so my position on this is never going to be as well informed as someone who lives it, but I have done a lot of research and learning on this, not to mention around 90% of all the clients I have ever worked with are female.

So, let's dig into it. Your cycle is broken down into two clear phases each with a further two phases within them.
The Follicular phase and the Luteal phase.
The Follicular phase is as you go from being on your period, through to proliferative phase and into ovulation.
The Luteal phase takes you from ovulation through to the secretary phase as you head towards your next period.

Where you are in these phases will drastically, for some especially, impact how you feel and perform. Which will play a huge role on your fat loss success.

Now as you head into ovulation and through into the Luteal phase you can expect to feel at your best.
It's often when you have the best levels of self esteem and confidence, highest sex drive, best strength and performance in the gym and life just feels good!

It is at this point of your cycle that it will be easiest to see progress and stay in a deficit. Your body is working in perfect harmony with you, you feel good, it feels good and your view of the world is great.

When you train you feel at your best and will often see personal bests being hit in this two week window.

However, as you head through your Luteal phase back towards your period you will see a few things happen.

Firstly, your energy levels and performance will begin to dip a little. Training can be a little harder and you notice you fatigue a little easier.
As you get your period there will be significant change.

A big factor in this is you could be burning up to 30% more calories at rest due to being on your period. This is a massive factor in why women often have low mood, no energy, low self esteem and body image issues during their period. Their hormones are making them feel pretty shitty and to cap it all off they're actually burning way more calories than they realise compounding how they feel.

But surely if you're burning more at rest that's good for fat loss, right? Well, no, not really.
What we tend to see is that increased appetite, lower mood and low energy ends up causing irregular food cravings and eating behaviours. All too often the calories are boosted up through very calorie dense food so you feel better, in turn taking you over your calories and out of a deficit.
This then compounds the low mood as you feel you're failing and self sabotaging.

But, hear me out… you're actually not.
Yes, going over calories for a week due to your period may slightly slow progress but in truth if you're maximising the 3

weeks of the month you feel pretty good then the likelihood is you'll still be averaging a deficit over the course of the month. This is exactly why I encourage all my female clients, if needed, to increase calories back to maintenance for the week of their period. For many that's an extra 500kcals per day allowing for more food, to better manage hunger and also allows more of the calorie dense foods they usually feel guilty for eating.

This actually enables them to feel better both physically by getting more calories in and mentally as they're not feeling like a failure for eating what they're craving at a time their body needs more calories.

Another factor that hugely impacts how you feel you're doing is what happens on the scales during your period.
Your body will be holding a lot more water than usual, could be as much as 5kg more!

What often happens is women weigh themselves the week of their period and feel shit that they've gone backwards. My first advice is to not weigh yourself for that week.
If you want to though, make a note that it is your period and instead of comparing to the previous week, compare to the last time you had your period.
This is because you may have gone up since last week, but if you're lighter than your last period that is still progress.

More often than not people just compare back to the week before and feel like they worked really hard but gained weight when the reality is you're holding water, water that will be gone in a few days. So, if you want to compare against anything only compare it against your last period.

Now, as you come off your period and head back towards ovulation what you all see is a gradual improvement to your energy, performance, strength, mood and your body getting rid of all that stored water.

It is important that when thinking about fat loss we understand it is the result of consistent long term action. If we know one week in every 4 isn't going to be ideal conditions for us to prioritise fat loss and being in a deficit then what is much more logical is to adjust the plan to reflect this and allow for it rather than trying to ignore the inevitable and creating the risk that you feel like you're failing.

If you focus on your efforts for the three weeks you are essentially at your best and then make contingencies for the week of your period you will make it far more likely you will succeed long term.
Obviously increasing calories is a big part but I would also seek to implement a deload week for your period too. This simply means making everything much less intense.
If you're weight training, drop all the weights down to lighter weights and seek volume. By not trying to lift heavy you won't feel annoyed if there's strength decreases. The change in approach will help you mentally and physically as it gives a bit of variety to your training.
If you're not weight training and are more cardio based, take a similar approach and go for more low intensity, steady state cardio, often known as LISS (more about that later). By working at a lower intensity, you will be able to still feel you're doing something worthwhile without feeling frustrated by any lack of energy or performance that comes from being on your period.

If you do this you will ensure that you keep on top of things and over the course of a month will still be doing more than enough to drive significant change without feeling like every time you make progress your own body holds you back.

But what happens as you get older and your cycles become less regular and you head into perimenopause or menopause?

Well, this can have a significant impact too. The biggest impacts are that changes in your hormone production can result in a significant reduction of the amount of calories you burn at rest. This is often why women feel they haven't changed anything but begin to gain weight.
When you add to this the fact that you will also see increased rates of sarcopenia, muscle loss, that too will contribute to burning less calories at rest.
So, what can you do?

My best advice is to be patient, fat loss may take a little longer, but it's better to take longer than to go backwards or make your life fucking miserable, after all the hormonal fluctuations can make you feel bad enough as it is.

Couple being patient with increasing your activity level, ideally with resistance training so you can hold onto and potentially grow as much muscle as possible to offset the sarcopenia and therefore increase the calories burned at rest.
With this you will also want to bring more focus to protein to aid that maintenance and growth of muscle as well as increasing the calories burned at rest through the thermic effect of food.

Many of my clients are peri or menopausal and still lose body fat, whilst enjoying life. It just takes a recalculation of your calories, consistency and patience as it may well take longer than your used to.
But I promise you, it is not impossible! The answer simply is to avoid doing anything drastic as that will likely make you feel much worse.

There are other issues that women can face that will impact how you feel and your progress.

PCOS for example. This can make life feel very difficult from a fat loss perspective. This is due to, like menopause, a reduction in the calories burned at rest and fluctuations in hormones affecting how you feel.

Much like during your period our menopause the key there is to adopt a process that isn't too demanding and ultimately takes into account the fact you will be burning less calories at rest.

Increasing protein, including resistance training and being a little more patient are fairly important to offsetting any impacts PCOS is having on your body.

another area that often affects more women than men is thyroid issues. Again, the knock on effect here is usually a reduction in the calories burned at rest so much like everything else we need to offset that with the right approach and an adjustment of our expectations around the speed of progress.

The key thing to understand is that your period, PCOS, peri/menopause, thyroid issues etc. do not play outside the realms of physics. Meaning if you're seeking fat loss, you still simply need to eat less calories than you burn.

The bit that needs thought is to calculate what a deficit actually looks like, as you may need a larger one than before or to shift the expectations of how fast progress should come. It is also worth noting you may want to focus less on your weight and more on measurements and performance as a guide to your progress.

What I can promise is that, even if you feel it's impossible, it really isn't you just need to find the right approach, something I am confident this book will help with.

A challenge we all face, no matter what our gender, is falling into the trap of seeking out what we want to hear rather than aiming to find the truth.
We can all be guilty of ignoring things we don't like the sound of or that contradict our own opinions.
This can be a real inhibitor to progress and is exactly what we will discuss now.

Confirmation Bias.

It is not uncommon in the world of fat loss for people to dispute the importance of a calorie deficit and its role in fat loss.
In fact, many people make their living off of trying to dispute this and it is important to analyse why this is done as well as break down the truth behind the matter.

For a large swathe of people who try to dispute the calories in vs calories out message, they do so because they want to 'stand out' from the crowd. They want to sound more compelling and ultimately want to find a way to keep you at arms length from the truth, as we explored earlier in the book when looking at the principle vs the method.

There are some incredible people out there who are investigating all manner of areas such as performance who also, through isolated studies of very specific processes may also hypothesise other elements that are at play when it comes to fat loss.

The challenge here, with both of these groups is they tend to allow their own beliefs and experiences to overshadow what the data actually tells them.

When this happens, even if it is through scientific exploration and experimentation people stop looking to discover what the outcome of a study is and start trying to deliver their desired outcome by adjusting the study.

It is why so many fad diets exist, where there are so many people who claim insulin management is key for fat loss, why certain types of cardio is better and it is even why we have these generational phases where certain foods are demonised as the cause of fat gain or certain approaches and food are glamorised as the key to fat loss.

When this happens the people involved are putting their opinions ahead of the facts in order to find something that backs up what they think, and ultimately shows them what they want to see.

What makes it challenging is that whilst all calories are equal, in that 1 calorie is always 1 calorie, not all calories are absorbed the same by the body.
Much like a mile uphill is much harder and will feel longer than a mile downhill it is entirely possible for food to be absorbed totally differently.
For example, 100kcal of potato vs 100kcal of chicken.
It's the same amount of calories, but the potato (carbs) will be broken down into energy to fuel training, or refuel muscles that have just been trained. Whereas the chicken (protein) will be broken down into amino acids to repair the same muscles. Each process will burn a different amount of calories to metabolise therefore having a different impact on the body.
It's the same amount of calories, processed differently.
However, despite these different roles for different foods, and

there are complexities between foods and how they're used, one thing still remains constant.
Fat loss is always governed by calories in vs calories out. Irrespective of how your body breaks down those calories the key thing is in order to lose fat, you have to be eating less than you burn.

So, where does confirmation bias come into all this? Simply put, people who either truly believe or are positioning a belief to hide the principle, will always seek to find other information that confirms what they think and they will disregard anything that disputes this belief.
You will find that in order to maintain their standpoint they will cherry pick studies, often only pulling out very specific elements of studies to make their point as well as further confirming their belief. Some people go as far as to conducting studies designed to prove a specific outcome rather than seeking to see what the outcome is, just so they can maintain their view and get the dopamine hit that comes from getting their confirmation bias.

In short, confirmation bias is ignoring the overwhelming facts by seeking small bits of information that match your opinion. Usually driven by an emotional attachment to what has worked for you and it always is in complete denial of fact.
Think Flat Earthers, there's thousands of people who, despite all the overwhelming evidence against them, still believe the world to be flat.
The diet industry is full of people doing just this, the difference being most of them are doing so in order to make money off the back of what they're saying. Some genuinely believe it others actually know what they're saying isn't true but also know it sounds compelling enough to be believable. I call those people, shitcunts.

The issue is, people will more often than not believe what they want to believe. To the point they will only seek out the information they want to see in order to justify their belief. Personally, I try to find information that proves me wrong and research its credibility to make sure that what I say is actually evidence based and the truth.

In the diet world all the information around fad diets and dieting protocols is often far more anecdotal than factual. Lots of studies will examine what happened when eating in certain ways and following certain diets without actually drawing your attention to the actual calorie intake.
What's worse is most so called fit pros will have a method they make their clients adopt that have always *'worked'*. These are often methods for creating a deficit but by adopting a *'my client did this, and it worked'* only serves to feed into their confirmation bias and to bolster their opinion that their method is the only way to elicit fat loss.

By seeking to reaffirm their beliefs it then allows them to feed that information to you enforcing their own confirmation bias onto you the consumer.

When you break it all down and look at the actual evidence out there one thing is clear.
No matter what someone's belief is on fat loss the only actual way to elicit it is to create a calorie deficit.
Many people will have differing views on the best way to do this but the data shows very little superiority from one method to the next and the underlying and overriding factor is the management of calorie intake.

People pushing opinions on the best approach, exercise, diet or even TV or Netflix documentaries positioning opinions as fact are quite simply that.

Opinions.

Someone's view on the subject that is being positioned strongly in the hope you adhere to their approach.

So, when it comes to finding the best method for you, be careful. Do your research and pay close attention to what people are saying. I guarantee most people pushing a strong opinion, seeking to enforce their own confirmation bias onto you will do so through many anecdotes and stories of other people's success rather than an outpouring of overwhelming evidence to substantiate their claims.

After all, as Ricky Gervais once said;

"We shouldn't be changing the facts to match people's opinions. People should change their opinions to match what the facts tell us."

Confirmation bias is the exact opposite, and is a leading reason why there is so much conflicting information out there surrounding fat loss.

What I can say is before embarking on any approach, don't get swept up in how many people have done it and seen results. Look at how it works, understand how it will create a deficit and if that is a method you wish to adopt and can stick to long term, whilst enjoying it.

After all, just because a million people are doing something fucking stupid it doesn't stop it being something stupid. It just means there's a million stupid people doing it.
I am sure you don't want to be one of them.

Which brings me nicely onto the next section where I will take you through all the fads out there and how they actually work.

Fad Diets.

Every pound of fat ever lost has been done so through the existence of a calorie deficit, which is exactly what a fad diet creates but doesn't want you to know.

The reason why fad diets don't work long term is simply because they don't teach you anything about how they work or how to maintain them. They simply pinpoint one food group or behaviour and tell you to remove it. In the short term this works a treat but in reality, the behaviour or food group is not something you can cope without for the long term so what ends up happening is this;
You follow it for a while and see some progress, sometimes rapid progress.
You then begin to want to do the one thing it says you can't until you can't say no anymore.
The diet then makes you feel like a failure so you quit and go back to *'normal'* meaning all progress is lost.
You wait a while and when you feel sick of how you look and want to effect change again you reach for what *'worked'* before or another fad and repeat the cycle.

If you break down every diet all they actually do is create a deficit the trouble is, to make them a one size fits all effort the deficit is usually huge. Hence the rapid results you often see at the beginning, meaning you will quit in no time. This isn't necessarily to make you fail but more because for it to work for the majority of people it has to be extreme, if it wasn't it wouldn't work for a lot of people.

The key to fat loss is actually establishing what is best for you as an individual, not a one size fits all approach because in the history of everything one size has never actually fitted all, because of the 8billion people on the planet no two are the same!

So, if we look at each fad in turn, we can see how they create a deficit, we can also see that the deficit is what they all have in common along with the fact it is a very unsustainable approach, check this out;

Keto - Cut out an entire food group, therefore creating a deficit by removing 1/3 of what you eat. Often coupled with Intermittent fasting, so you also remove 1/3 of your meals. Eating less food quantity and less meals will help create a deficit but if you like the food group you're told not to eat and don't like fasting it'll suck really fast! Not to mention removing carbs results in huge amounts of water loss, through the depletion of glycogen in your muscles, which is why when you cut carbs you lose a lot in the first couple of weeks. This is not fat loss but often creates the illusion that the diet is working.

Intermittent fasting - This is literally shortening your eating window by removing a meal and bringing meals into a shorter time frame. This can help, less meals can mean less food, not eating after a certain time too can mean less calories. But if you still eat the same food just closer together during the day you will still be eating too many calories. Equally if shorter eating windows doesn't suit your lifestyle, it simply won't be something you can stick to.

Meal replacement shakes - Swapping eating food for drinking it instead. Whilst this can help calorie control the meals you replace, if you're over consuming at the other meals it'll do fuck all and most people end up eating more when they do eat simply as they feel unsatisfied from drinking their calories earlier in the day.

Juice detoxes - You're literally blending your food instead of eating it, much like meal replacement shakes this is pointless if you're not controlling the calories you actually consume and eat. It's also highly unfulfilling so is likely to become unsustainable quickly and lead to increased calorie consumption later in the day.

You can see where I am going with this. There are many other diets out there I haven't mentioned but, they all create a deficit by telling you to not eat something. They also neglect to tell you that the reason for not eating whatever it is they say to avoid is to create a deficit.
The big question is;
How long can you realistically not eat that for?
If you really like it, you might avoid it a few weeks but not long. Also, we shouldn't be demonising certain foods or eating behaviours, as no foods are good or bad.
When trying to drop fat you need to have an approach you can stick to and enjoy long term.
If a diet sounds like it'll suck before you start, you'll quit in a matter of weeks.
If a diet includes the food, you like but helps you manage calorie intake in line with you goal you won't even realise, you're on a diet and will create a lifestyle that works for you long term.

That is the key to long term fat loss progress. It's not about rapid results, after all you didn't get into this situation in matter of weeks. It has been months, if not years, of overeating that led to a need for change.
So, rather than kidding yourself into thinking you can do something shit for a few weeks and reach your goals, just focus on making easy to implement, simple to stick to and enjoyable changes to your lifestyle and watch you change your life for good.

In Summary.

In short, when it comes to your nutrition my best piece of advice to each and every person is this.

You need to eat less calories than you burn, how you go about that, what food you choose to eat, when you choose to eat it is entirely down to you and your own preference.

Your long term success will come down to how much you can enjoy your chosen approach and how long you can realistically do it for.

If you make an enormous amount of change that you can only hope to stick to short term, don't expect to keep your results long term. After all a short term fix to a long term problem is never going to work out.

The real key is including the food you enjoy, eating as close to what you would consider to be *'normally'* as possible whilst managing calories in line with your expenditure. Why?
Well because if you stick to it long enough to reach your goal you will want to bring yourself out of a deficit at some point. There is no benefit to changing your life so much that when you want to maintain your results it requires yet another significant change.

In fact, what you want to aim for is being able to make minimal changes to what you eat, only increasing the amount of calories up to your new maintenance in order to maintain your results for one, but also to ensure as little disruption to your lifestyle as possible as you transition out of a deficit. Because, if there is one thing, I can confirm its this; Transitioning from a deficit to maintenance or even a small surplus can be a head fuck. A head fuck that is made all the more easier if it doesn't require another wholesale change to your diet and lifestyle.

So, before you start obsessing over should you cut out sugar, go keto, how long should you fast, do you need to go vegan, go carnivore, join Slimming World, use meal replacement shakes, do smoothies, juice cleanses or any other bullshit take one big step back.

Stop, take a breath and ask yourself this one simple question.

"Do I know how many calories I actually need to be eating?" If you don't know the answer to that then you really should start there.
Once you know what your average calorie target should be it becomes easier to decide what approach is going to be best to get you there.

If you need a hand calculating your calories my website has a free calorie calculator you can use -
www.redefineacademy.com/calorie-calculator

My guess is it won't be through doing any of the above and it will be through managing your calorie intake whilst including the food you actually enjoy eating.

So don't get caught up in the fads, the bullshit and blind yourself with misinformation. Stick to the basics and trust the process.

Fat loss shouldn't be a slog so if you can't see yourself enjoying the process a year from now don't adopt that method. I will talk more about the mindset needed much later on in the book but when it comes to nutrition this is the foundation of your success, so adopting a method you can actually enjoy is key to long term success.

Because, remember this.

The man who enjoys the journey will travel further than the man who simply enjoys the destination.

This completes the nutrition side of things and whilst our diet is the most important element to eliciting fat loss it is imperative not to overlook the significant role played by training and exercise.

After all, there is still around 20% of our total calories burned that come from activity in general and whilst only 5% is from your training, training delivers so many other benefits to altering your physique above just burning calories.

So, let's take a good look at it now.

Section 2
Calories Out

Training.

Training is a vital component when it comes to making progress and altering your overall body composition. It should form a foundation of your lifestyle, not just from a fat loss perspective but also from a general health perspective.

In this section of the book, I will talk you through how our bodies burn energy, the different training modalities out there and the benefits of each as well as helping break down some of the myths and misconceptions associated with training.

After all training isn't just about getting ripped and turning into Bulk Hogan or Lord Swoldermort.
There are actually way more significant benefits to training above and beyond the growth of muscle or the burning of calories.
Similarly, it's not all about slogging it out on the treadmill either.
Especially when fat loss is concerned, training forms a fundamental element for your success.
But wait, didn't I say earlier that training only burns 5% of our daily calories and you can't out-train a bad diet?
You fucking bet I did and this section explains exactly what I mean by that and why viewing your training as simply a way to burn calories is about as pointless as burning your cash so you don't spend it.

Training vs Exercising

Before we dive headfirst into training and all that goes into it, I want to explore the difference between training and exercising.

But surely, they're the same thing? Well… in short, no, they're different in a number of ways.

Exercising is simply the art of burning calories, it is essentially more cardio based. I will go into this in a lot more detail later in this section.

Training however is way more than just burning calories. Training is the constant pursuit of progress and performance improvements. Training your body is to seek to improve it. Be that from a strength, size, speed, agility or stamina based perspective.

Training isn't just doing a little exercise, training is adopting a process to follow, it's seeing how much your body is capable of.

Exercise is important, it can be enjoyable and you can see progress in it too. I'm not for a second saying that exercise isn't worth doing by any stretch.
But there is a significant difference between the two.
Many people adopt a cardio based approach when seeking fat loss thinking they need to burn as many calories as possible and that doing cardio will get them dropping fat faster.
Not only is this not entirely true it also isn't a requirement like many people believe it to be.

In truth, if we look at what we can learn from exercise vs training it's clear to see why it's important to differentiate between the two.

Exercise teaches us to burn calories. To work harder to burn more calories. Which isn't a bad thing but it can become a bit toxic, not least when you realise you may not be burning as many calories as you think.

Training however teaches us discipline, consistency, patience and control. It teaches us that we can get better at something with time. We can change our bodies without focusing purely on burning calories. It teaches us the importance of following a process as well as improving muscle mass, bone density, balance as well as our confidence and self belief.

In short, training is just as much about our mindset and behaviours as it is about our bodies and when we train, we gain way more than just burning some calories. Sure, we do that too but what we gain from training is way more than just calories burned.

So, before we explore the different forms of training and exercise let's take a look at how our body actually burns energy.

Energy Systems.

Now, as I said, before I dig into all things training it is important to understand how our bodies burn energy, this will become clear why later in this section.
But our bodies use two main fuel sources Fats and Carbs. Imagine your body is like a hybrid car, fats are the battery and carbs are the petrol.
Fats, aka the battery, are fine for travelling around town at lower speeds. Much like fats are great for low intensity steady state training.
Carbs, however, are like the petrol. When you pull onto the motorway and need to stick your foot down or you want to make some little prick in a fiesta look like a bellend at the lights, petrol is what's delivering the explosive power. That is how we use carbs, when we need explosive energy quickly in short bursts our body will use carbs.

Our body loves burning carbs as its far easier and way more explosive but neither is better than the other, in fact they just have different purposes.

Which is why when people tell you to go low carb and high fat to 'burn more fat' they're misleading you. You'll burn more fat from an energy perspective but it isn't more superior for a fat loss point of view, for fat loss it's less about what energy source or system we're using and all about are we burning more calories than we're consuming.

Now, there is a lot more we could cover on energy systems with regards to the role of creatine, ATP and ADP and a lot of stuff you learn in GCSE PE or when doing your PT qualifications about how the body switches between systems and produces energy etc. but from a fat loss perspective you just don't need to know this. This is because you can't control this stuff, your body manages that for you, so why worry about it?

All you need to know is you can use either fats or carbs for energy and a combination of both is probably best as you'll use each a little differently. So, there is little benefit or need to reduce carbs if fat loss is the goal. *Cough, **fuck keto**, cough*.

It is also worth acknowledging that when in a deficit consistently the body will burn stored fat but can also burn muscle mass too. Which is why it is essential to not take calories too low and to maintain high amounts of protein to negate this as much as possible.

After all those in comas don't just lose fat, they lose muscle too, otherwise they'd all be coming out of their comas looking like the Rock!

Since that doesn't happen it is fair to say our body will use muscle and fat for energy when in a deficit so to ensure we minimise the loss of muscle as much as possible we need to keep protein high and ideally include resistance training.

This is different to burning fats and carbs for energy release, this is more about what the body will breakdown when calorie intake is consistently lower than calorie expenditure. Ensuring calories are not taken too low, protein intake is kept high and resistance training forms part of your weekly routine will minimise the loss of muscle mass when in a deficit. Not least because the amount of muscle you hold not only enables you to burn more calories at rest but also because it will have a significant impact on your physique, aesthetically, as you get leaner.

Resistance training yields so many benefits, which will be covered in more detail shortly but ensuring we are holding and retaining good amounts of muscle are key for fat loss, as previously discussed.

Before we get into training in more detail let's explore the two ways our body burns calories from activity in a more detail.

NEAT

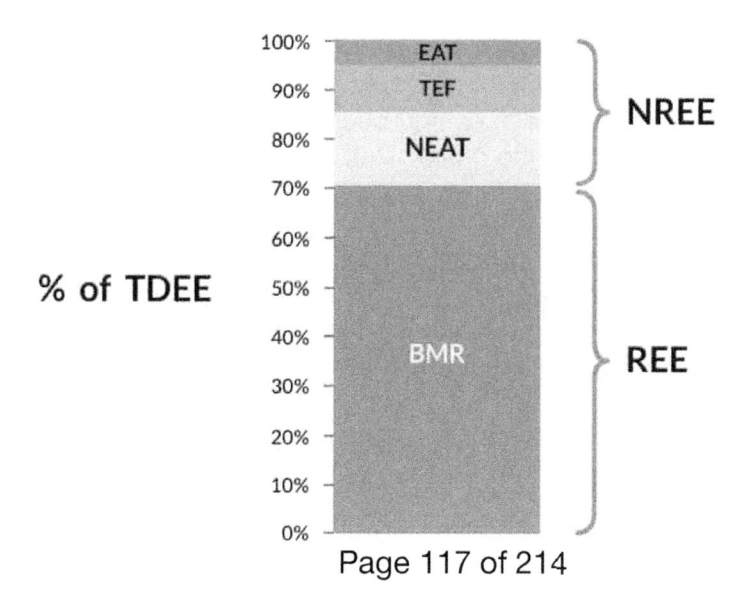

You may have heard of NEAT; you should remember it from earlier in the book in truth, but NEAT is one of the most important tools in your arsenal when it comes to making progress with fat loss. This is because it makes up the second largest portion of where we burn calories each day! NEAT stands for Non-Exercise Activity Thermogenesis. On average, NEAT, makes ups around 15% of the calories we burn each day and it includes every form of movement we conduct daily that isn't planned exercise.

One of the biggest contributors to increasing our NEAT, and one of the easiest ways to up it, is through an effective step count.
Now, you may have heard fit pros bang on about hitting your 10k steps each day.
This isn't because 10k is the magic number for steps that causes fat to just fall off our bodies, in fact there is no real 'science' behind 10k other than the fact it requires a conscious effort to hit and if you're doing 10k steps you'll be burning a very good amount of calories from that step count.

Some people get a little vexed with whether a step count is actually planned activity or non planned if you're 'planning in' time to go for a walk each day and to this is say…
Fuck me pal, there's more important things to worry about than if your steps are planned or unplanned. In fact, I would look at it this way - steps counts and walks are 'unplanned' exercise that just form part of your day to day routine. In gym and at home workouts are your planned exercise. If you view it that way you are far less likely to get all confused on what counts as what and in reality, it doesn't fucking matter, if you're burning calories and becoming more active… that's the whole point so who really gives a flying fuck if it's 'planned' or 'unplanned'.

The point very much still remains by increasing general activity during the day you will burn more calories without putting too much pressure on your actual training, because there is way more to training than just burning calories!

Some simple ways to increase your NEAT are;

Spend less time sat down, standing burns more calories than sitting so spend less time sat on your ass.

More steps, which I know is unhelpful on its own but ways to up your steps are parking further from the shop, walking instead of driving to places that are within walking distance. Making sure you get up and walk around once every hour, this can be very helpful if you spend your day sat at a desk!

Take the stairs not the escalator. In fact, it's crazy that escalators give you the ability to get somewhere quicker. If you walk up an escalator, you'll reach the top much quicker than taking the stairs but people are so fucking lazy that rather than get there quicker they see escalators as a chance to stand still! So, take the stairs next time!

The reality is most people are fairly sedentary in their day to day lives and finding ways to change that, even just for 10 minutes per day can play a significant role in aiding fat loss. Not least because the more active you are in general, the more calories you will burn in general meaning it will be easier to adhere to a calorie deficit.

Think about it this way, we know around a 500kcal deficit is a decent size deficit each day to achieve sustainable fat loss. If you're TDEE totals 2,000kcal your calorie target for a deficit will be 1,500kcal, which for a lot of people will feel too low. If you can increase activity to burn an extra 500kcals per day your target calories for a deficit would increase by 500kcals too meaning you'd be on 2,000kcal per day and still in a deficit. Something that will be far easier to stick to. It's the same size deficit but a higher calorie target will be far easier to adhere to.

Now, whilst it is unlikely you will burn 500kcal per day just by upping your steps, when you become more active you do make it easier on yourself to stay in a deficit by increasing the amount you can eat each day, and let's face it, no one wants to live off poverty calories.

So, making a conscious effort to walk more, spend less time sat down and just move more throughout the day will all help you burn more calories without even having to think about it. This is precisely why making sure you're as active as you can be throughout the day can be a huge contributor to success and helps you create a much more active lifestyle without feeling like you're going out of your way to do so!

Whilst NEAT makes up a significant block of the calories we burn each day and the leading amount of calories burned from activity it is essential we also look at how many calories we burn from our planned exercise, our EAT.

EAT.

Exercise activity thermogenesis, often abbreviated to EAT, is essentially what we call all of our planned exercise.
The best way to view this, to avoid any confusion with NEAT is this is your planned training that you are aiming to do each week, that ultimately your calorie target will be calculated based upon.
Unlike NEAT, which will be fairly consistent day to day. Your EAT may vary slightly day by day and week on week but almost everyone will have a target for the number of days per week they can train.
My advice with this is to air on the side of caution when deciding how many days per week you're aiming to train.

This is because when calculating your calorie deficit, it will be calculated based on your TDEE, and whilst EAT only makes up around 5% of the calories you burn each week, it still plays a significant role in ensuring you're in a deficit.

This is why going from never training to trying to train every day of the week is usually a recipe for disaster. Having such a drastic change of lifestyle is usually something people can only keep up for a short period of time. The other issue is if you're deficit is dependent on you training 5 times per week but you can realistically only make it there 2-3 times, you'll be eating far too many calories for the amount you actually move. This is why, when getting started, it is always better to be more conservative with your expectations of how active you will be.

Consider this, if you aim for five days but consistently go three, you will be eating too many calories for one but also be feeling like a failure each and every week making it more likely that you quit. Sound familiar? The classic *"This is too much; I can't do it!"*.

Now, flip that on its head. You aim to go twice and base your calorie target all on training twice per week but find you actually begin going three times. It's the same amount of activity, three times per week, but firstly your calories will be in the right place, in fact you'll actually be burning more than expected. Secondly, you're going to feel like you're a fucking G because instead of going twice you're going thrice! It's the same amount of sessions per week but psychologically you feel so different about it.

Something I cover later in this book is mindset but one of the biggest factors to long term success is keeping yourself feeling like you're doing well, that is all to do with our mindset. Our mindset is largely dictated by our perception of how well we are doing so creating a plan, a lifestyle that actually works for us and doesn't demand more than we can give is a key factor to preserving a positive mindset.

When it comes to our training the harsh reality is that over the course of a week it doesn't burn as many calories as we believe it does. So, many people will look at a workout as though it can burn off a pizza or earn them a Chinese and a few beers.
This mindset is beyond flawed because a Pizza could easily hit 2,000kcals (if it's a large dominos stuffed crust especially) and a Chinese and beers could be just as much, or more. The challenge is that an intense 45 minute - 1 hour workout will burn in the region of 300-450kcals, depending on the person, intensity etc. When you take that into account it is clear to see why trying to use training as way to burn off or earn high calorie food is not likely to elicit the success, you're after.

Now, many of you burn probably closer to 300kcals in a session, if you're lucky. Whilst you might be sat there thinking hold on, 300kcals that's more than 5% of my TDEE. You would be correct. But if you only train 3 times per week that 300kcals per session equals 900kcals per week, when you divide that by 7 days it is an average of 128kcals per day burned from training activity. Which if you burn a total of 2,400kcals per day from your TDEE (which isn't a massive amount) it would only work out to be about 5%.

As mentioned above, a lot of people actually burn much less than they realise in a session, but in truth when it comes to your planned exercise the amount of calories you burn is one of the least exciting parts about training.

But I can't stress enough how important it is to be realistic with your expectations around training to ensure that you calorie target is correct and reflective of how active you actually will be rather than how active you think you need to be.

We can always increase over time, in fact it is always better to start small and get good at going once or twice for a month or so and then build on that, making training an enjoyable part of your day and weekly routine, but there is no pressure to actually train.

A good step count and the right calories can still be more than enough to get you to your goals!
But what if you do train frequently and then suffer an injury or illness that means your activity is reduced?

My recommendation here is simple, how long will it be reduced by? Knowing your planned activity makes up around 5-10% of the calories you burn almost everyone can get away with a week or two of no activity without adjusting calories and still make progress.

The caveat to this is if it is more long term, you will probably want to recalculate your calorie target based on your new expenditure. This is something I wish I knew before I was qualified. I had been working on a progressive lean bulk and suffered a two year battle with tendonitis in my patella tendon (knee). It crippled my ability to train properly and my activity dropped from 4 down to 2 sessions per week. Suffice to say I kept eating like I was training 4 times per week and ended up piling the pounds on in two years.
Had I have adjusted my calories to reflect my new activity level I'd have been fine, so obviously if you're dealing with an injury or illness that will rumble on beyond a couple of weeks it will make sense to reduce calories a small amount to keep you on track.

So, with all this in mind, what's more important to focus on, NEAT or EAT?
Let's have a look.

NEAT vs EAT.

The age old battle, the great debate… which is better NEAT or EAT? - There's only one way to find out… no, not fight!
In reality there is no 'this is better than that'. They both play a significant role in changing your overall body composition they just do it in different ways.

As we know, EAT is all about our training, and our training should be about more than burning calories, not least because it doesn't burn anywhere near as many as we would like.
This doesn't mean it is less important that's for sure. The correct training stimulus is key for your goal, as I will discuss shortly, but if you have specific performance based goals or aesthetic based goals your training is going to be a key element to achieving them. It is part of a very important pyramid of importance when it comes to changing your composition or achieving your performance based goals, there's more on this later.

NEAT is more of a competent for general health and activity. It is a key player in creating a lifestyle that keeps you active and actually eases the pressure on your training from a fat loss perspective. It also makes staying in a deficit substantially easier by ensuring you burn more calories throughout the day which in turn means you can eat slightly more calories and still be in the same size deficit. And believe me being able to eat 1800 rather than 1500 makes a huge difference.

So where should we be putting our focus if fat loss is the goal?
In truth, the best results will come from both, BUT!! If you want my advice, which given you bought this book you clearly fucking do…

If fat loss is your goal the simple, easiest and most effective change you can make to your life to aid your progress is to increase your NEAT.
There is a reason that a certain Diren Kartal reached insta fame from promoting #NEATup247, because he is very much correct.
Increasing how active you are in general, walking more, spending less time sat on your ass and just trying your best to be as active as you can will make your life so much easier.
As we know NEAT makes up around 15% of what you burn in a day, if you increase it, it takes the pressure off of having to workout so fucking intensely.
This isn't me saying don't workout! Far from it, but your workouts, realistically, should be about more than just how many calories you burn in a session.
If you are hitting a good step count each day of 10,000 or more it means the focus of your training can shift from being a calorie burning exercise to actually focusing on improving your overall fitness level, getting stronger, improving balance and ultimately can become performance and aesthetic focused. This then means the calories you burn in training can just be a happy little bonus.

Plus, for many people finding time to train as hard as they would like can be a challenge. For the parents with kids, a busy job, a home to clean, pets to walk etc. finding time to train can be fucking hard work whereas getting your steps in can be done throughout the day without much disruption.

So, when it comes to NEAT or EAT… start with a good step count, because, as I have said, you'll be amazed what can be achieved with the right calories and a good step count. Once you feel comfortable with increasing your NEAT look to bring some sessions into the mix too, if you're really new to things.

Because there is no benefit to thinking you can, or have to, train 5 times per week if you have never trained before and are realistically unlikely to be able to train that much. You can always improve on what you're doing, over time, so start small.

"It is better to move at 1mph in the correct direction, than 100mph in the wrong direction".

In fact, trying to place too much dependance on training in the gym and being overly ambitious are two of the biggest reasons people ultimately give up on their goals in the early stages.

So, focus on increasing your NEAT, get good at that and gradually include training overtime and you'll be less overwhelmed and there will be less of a focus on your training being about burning calories which will make the sessions about a million times more enjoyable *(that figure is in no way shape or form made up…)*.
So, with this in mind let's take a look at the different training styles.

Training Styles.

When it comes to training there are a number of ways you can exercise and whilst they fall into an almost endless list of categories and subcategories of different disciplines and modalities, the best way to break them down is into two main groups, each with a number of subsets.

Training essentially falls into either Cardiovascular Training, often referred to as cardio or Resistance Training. In short training either works your cardiovascular system or it works your muscles. Yes, some do a bit of both, but either way all training styles will prioritise one of those two elements above the other.

Now within each of these are many different approaches and exercises, there are also training styles that bridge the gap between the two and combine elements of each.

When working out which style is best for you there are a number of factors to consider but the two most important are your goals specifically from an aesthetic perspective and from a performance perspective and then there is the factor of enjoyment.
What you will actually enjoy doing plays a huge role in if you can incorporate it into your daily lifestyle and therefore stick to it long enough to see results.

When it comes to your goals, if you have specific aesthetic or performance based goals you have to ensure your training style will actually elicit that response. There is no benefit to doing hours of cardio if your goal is to grow your ass or chest. Equally if your goal is to improve your marathon time there is much less benefit to spending hours in the weights room.

In truth which style of training, or training modality you adopt should really include both cardio and resistance training ideally, for optimum health, but as I said a highly significant factor has to be enjoyment because if you hate how, you train you simply won't stick to it.

People all too often get swept along with what they think is going to be best for their overall goal. Many people seeking fat loss do hours of cardio thinking it will make them lose fat quicker. Similarly, many people fall into traditional weight training programs thinking it will make them look like Hulk Hogan without truly understanding the key elements of their actual goal and how to apply a training approach that supports that.

What you want to achieve and how you want to look will ultimately dictate how you need to train, that being said your approach still needs to be one you're going to actually enjoy otherwise you won't stick to it.

So, let's look into some of the details around training so you can get an idea of what each style delivers to help work out what you will enjoy and need to do, starting with cardio.

Cardio.

Cardio is often people's first thought and 'go to' exercise style when fat loss is sought, largely due to the fact you can burn the most amount of calories doing cardio. But let's face it there has to be more to life, and fat loss for that, than hours on the treadmill.
After all, you're not a fucking hamster on a wheel!

Cardio is still very important, but not for the amount of calories you can burn but for the improvements to your overall health and the strength of your heart and lung capacity for example.
In fact, some of the more significant benefits to cardio above and beyond the amount of calories burned are;
Improvements to cardiovascular health,
Increased blood flow,
Greater lung capacity,
More endurance,
Improved stamina, in and out of the bedroom,
Released endorphins improving mood, to name but a few.

In fact, cardio is way more than just burning calories, not least because you don't actually burn as many as you might think and when it comes to cardio there are so many different options out there besides just getting on the old treadmill.

You have;
Walking,
Jogging,
Running,
Cycling,
Swimming,

Climbing,
Shagging,
Playing sports,
Cross trainer,
Stairmaster,
Rowing machine,
HIIT Cardio,
LISS Cardio.

I am sure there are even more forms of cardio but let's face it, you're not here for me to simply list them all.

When it comes to cardio you have two main approaches, you have High Intensity Interval Training (also known as HIIT) and you have Low Intensity Steady State (also known as LISS). Despite what some people will claim about HIIT, it actually isn't more superior to LISS or any other training styles for that. So, if you're forcing yourself through the ringer with your HIIT sessions because it's great for fat loss… think again. Do something you enjoy instead!

Regardless of if you're going balls to the wall for a little bit, resting and going again or plodding along more leisurely for an extended period of time my first piece of advice is this; Do your cardio outside! The gym may have lots of cardio equipment but you shouldn't be paying £30 per month (on average) to do something you can do outside, for free, in much nicer surroundings. Now, obviously when the weather is shit the idea of going outside might not appeal in which case do it indoors in the dry and warm. But otherwise, the gym really shouldn't just be somewhere you go just to burn calories and go mind-numbingly insane and bored out of your fucking skull because if that's all you do there, I guarantee you will quit. And most people do quit because they don't enjoy cardio and try to do an hour of it every day!

It is also worth highlighting that changing cardio machine every 5 or 10 minutes is a bit pointless too. Each machine will essentially help you raise your heart rate and burn calories, just pick the one you like the most and do that instead of jumping from machine to machine every 5 minutes, listing 10 machines used in a 40 minute session doesn't mean a more effective session in fact the time spent going from machine to machine probably means you'll burn less calories than if you stayed on one the entire time.

As for when you should be doing your cardio there are a number of studies that recommend, even when muscle growth is the goal, including cardio in your training plan will improve the rate in which you can up your weights when resistance training, meaning we should really have a combination of the two as part of our training plan.

But if that is the case, when should we do cardio in relation to weights?

If you can do them in separate sessions then definitely do that but for many of us, we don't have the time luxury to be able to train twice per day. So, if you're having to do them in the same session here is my advice.

Do your heavy lifting first. Literally and metaphorically. Hitting your weights first when you have the most amount of energy and can maximise your lifts is always going to benefit you significantly.
Cardio can be done at a lower intensity at the end.
After all, if you're going to need to be explosive for your lifts you don't want to burn yourself out beforehand. This isn't like having one off the wrist before a date so that you last longer in the sack!

As always, there is a caveat to all this, if your goals are performance based, I.e., wanting to increase the time of your 10km run, the primary focus of your training should be cardio and prioritising your performance there.

If you goal is more aesthetically driven then it makes more sense to prioritise your weight training over cardio as that will drive far more impact on your body composition and overall aesthetics.

What about doing your cardio fasted or fed? Fasted cardio gets such a massive amount of publicity and some people get one hell of a stonk on over it too. Guess what though?
Fat loss is governed by your calorie intake not by your fed state when training. This means it is purely down to your own preference. In fact, if you do your cardio fasted or fed is more likely to be governed by the time of day you train and how you personally feel when doing cardio in the respective states rather than its effectiveness for fat loss.
If you need any reassurance, all of the studies exploring fasted vs fed state training, from a fat loss perspective, have all found the same thing.
When calories are matched the results are the same regardless of if the cardio is done in a fasted or fed state.
In short… do what you like best!

Ultimately, when it comes to cardio do what you enjoy and if you don't enjoy it don't force yourself to do it. Whilst it is good for you, when fat loss is concerned there is no requirement for any cardio at all. It can be a great tool without doubt but there is no actual hard and fast requirement so if you don't like it… don't fucking do it.
On the flip side, if you love it… knock yourself out!

Now, let's look at the fun stuff, resistance training!

Weights & Resistance Training

Now, many people (wrongly) assume resistance training is all about getting huge and only for the guys and girls who want to have massive muscles.
The truth is resistance training is one of the best forms of exercise we can incorporate into our lifestyle and it brings so many benefits beyond just building muscle that most people don't even realise.

Before we get into that, what is resistance training?
It is a training method that applies resistance to our movements.

There are many different disciplines to this that include;

Bodybuilding
Powerlifting
CrossFit
HIIT Resistance training.

Each has their own slightly different take on its structure but uses the addition of weights to build strength and endurance.

When it comes to lifting weights, with the intention of building muscle the response we are searching for from the body is hypertrophy, this is essentially where we put tears into the muscle fibre that can then rebuild and regrow, increasing the density of the fibres in the process.

For a long time, it was believed that in order to achieve this you had to do 3 sets of 10 reps however more recent studies have shown that hypertrophy can be achieved anywhere between 6-30 reps and that actually it is about training the muscles to around the point of failure to fatigue the muscles.

This actually means that you can, again, train more in line with enjoyment when it comes to rep ranges, something I will cover more of shortly.

When it comes to resistance training it carries so many benefits, especially with fat loss. The benefits include;

Improved balance,
Improved endurance,
Improved flexibility,
Improved bone density,
Increased muscle mass,
More calories burned at rest,
Delay sarcopenia (muscle loss as we get older)
Reduced risk of osteoporosis in later life,
Increased sex drive, sexual performance and stamina.

It is way more than getting swole. In fact, when compared to just doing cardio you will end up burning more calories from resistance training simply by the fact that when you train cardio you burn calories whilst you're training but within a few minutes of stopping and as your heart rate returns to normal you stop burning calories from an exercise standpoint.

With resistance training you burn calories during the session, but also more at rest due to the energy needed to recover and repair the muscles, as well as the fact that the more muscle mass you have the more calories you burn at rest too meaning it is a great way to increase the amount of calories you burn both during training but also at rest too.

And for those who worry that lifting weights will make them huge and muscly, I have some very positive news!
To add large amounts of muscle mass requires you to eat in a calorie surplus and train hard, as well as be very patient.

Without the use of steroids large amounts of muscle mass take months if not years to add and require being in a surplus. If you're in a calorie deficit and lifting weights 3 times per week you won't suddenly become massive, believe me I wish you could but it takes a lot of time and effort to gain size. However, what you will notice through lifting weight your body shape changes, you gain more confidence, you're happier and look fucking amazing!

Even more so than if you just do cardio, that is because many a person has lost a lot of weight doing cardio alone and still not felt like they loved their body. No one has ever lifted weights and lost fat and said they didn't love how they look. The reality is most people want to looked 'toned' and to achieve that you need to hold a good amount of muscle to show through as you lose fat, to achieve that… you need to lift weights.

That being said, whilst resistance training, including some cardio is optimum and would be my recommendation to everyone, enjoyment has to be a key component to how you train and if you simply hate resistance training maybe don't do it… unless your goal is to have a specific shape physique that can only be achieved through lifting… in that case you'll have to just learn to love it.

This does bring me nicely onto how often you should train and what volume you should be looking at.

Volume, Intensity & Frequency.

When it comes to training frequency and volume there are a lot of opinions floating about, often shared with a lot of conviction and belief that they are in fact facts. Remember what we said about confirmation bias!
Whilst there are some correlations between frequency and volume and certain goals it isn't an exact science and for fat loss, especially, I would still argue enjoyment and what is realistic should still form the basis for your volume and frequency.

Before I get into detail on this, I want to discuss what is meant by volume and frequency respectively.

Volume refers to the amount of exercises, reps and sets you're doing each session, basically this refers to how much you train a certain muscle group.

Intensity refers to how hard you are working in each session.

Frequency refers to how often you train each week.

When it comes to the frequency this will largely be dictated by how often you can actually train. There is no point in aiming to train each muscle group individually twice per week if you realistically can only train 2-3 times per week because you'll never achieve it. Now you could change up your training split to allow for say two full body sessions per week meaning each muscle group is hit twice per week but the trade off here will ultimately be the volume.

Yes, you can train each muscle group twice per week but if that's only one or two exercises per muscle group per session your total volume isn't very high, which could be detrimental to progress.

Ultimately your training frequency is going to be dictated by your lifestyle and how much time you can dedicate to training. My recommendation is if you can train three times per week look to train each muscle group well once per week. If you can go more, then sure, look to do more but three sessions per week is plenty and allows a good amount of volume and frequency.

When thinking about frequency, another factor to consider is recovery time between sessions. Realistically you don't want to be training the same muscle group two days in a row. In fact, I would aim for 2 days minimum between sessions on specific muscle groups.
When we train fatigued muscles, we risk injury and if you're resistance training specifically you will be pushing your muscles to the brink of failure and fatigue in a session so it is unwise to then train those same, tired, muscles the following day. Firstly, you risk injury but you will also reduce training performance as you're not allowing for adequate recovery before training again.

What you want to think about is getting the most out of your sessions. Maximising their effectiveness each and every time you step in the gym.
The gym isn't about burning calories, as we covered earlier, it's about improving performance and altering your body composition. For this you want to prioritise your performance over anything else. Adequate rest between sets and sessions is vital for optimum performance.
This doesn't just mean not training the same muscle group two days in a row but also taking adequate rest between sets. All too often people finish a set, pause for about 20 seconds tops and go again.

It's not a race! Equally, if you're able to go again almost immediately after stopping your set, and still hit your reps, you probably aren't training hard enough.
Your gym performance doesn't need to represent the training equivalent to how fast a 17 year old lad gets another boner after shooting a load.
So, train hard, take your rests between sets and maximise your performance,

This doesn't mean taking 5-10 minutes between sets either (unless you're powerlifting hitting your 1 rep max of course). Adequate rest should be around 1-3 minutes depending on intensity of your sets. A good gauge is around one and a half minutes. You want to ensure you rest enough to be able to perform well in the next set but not so much that it is like starting all over again.

As well as how long to rest, a lot of people struggle with knowing how much to lift. Often sticking to rep ranges even if the weight is too light or worse still sacrificing their form in order to do a certain number of reps with a weight that is way too heavy!

Before I get into how to combat that and how to gauge if you're working hard enough, I want you to consider this;

When it comes to building strength, you want to work with heavy weights falling into a rep range of 1-5 reps. Strength training or powerlifting isn't about building muscle, it is a different discipline to body building and as such you would work with heavier weight, lower rep ranges and longer rest periods to prioritise performance.

Bodybuilding or muscle building, i.e., building your physique (appearance) requires use to achieve muscle hypertrophy.

Hypertrophy comes from fatiguing the muscles and training in a fatigued state with adequate volume.
The rep ranges where we can achieve hypertrophy actually ranges from around 6-30 reps. So, whilst it is beneficial to lift heavy to build muscle as well you can actually achieve hypertrophy in larger rep ranges as well.

Now, irrespective of if you're resistance training for strength or muscle building purposes it is worth considering where the optimum training zone lies.

What you don't want to do, as previously mentioned, is stick to your rep ranges or weights at a detriment to your performance.

This is why I always recommend my clients work to a RPE or RIR. This stands for Rate of Perceived Exertion or Reps In Reserve.

A RPE relates to giving each set a score out of 10, 10 being the point you hit failure and 1 being very fucking easy.

Similarly, RIR is how many more reps you can realistically hit if you kept going.
An example of this would be an RPE of 8 or 2 RIR where you are aiming to hit your desired rep range with a maximum of 2 reps left in the tank before you hit failure, which would be about an 8 out of 10 for how hard the set is.

The below graph demonstrates this and where you want to aim for with your sets.
By focusing on leaving 2 reps in the tank or an RPE of 8 what you do is enable yourself to focus on your performance rather than the number of reps. Because we have all stopped at our desired reps when in reality we could do more.

Most of us have also completely sacrificed form just to get the last couple of reps out too making them fairly pointless. So, by adopting this approach you are more likely to gauge your training more effectively meaning you're less likely to sacrifice your form or your effort levels.

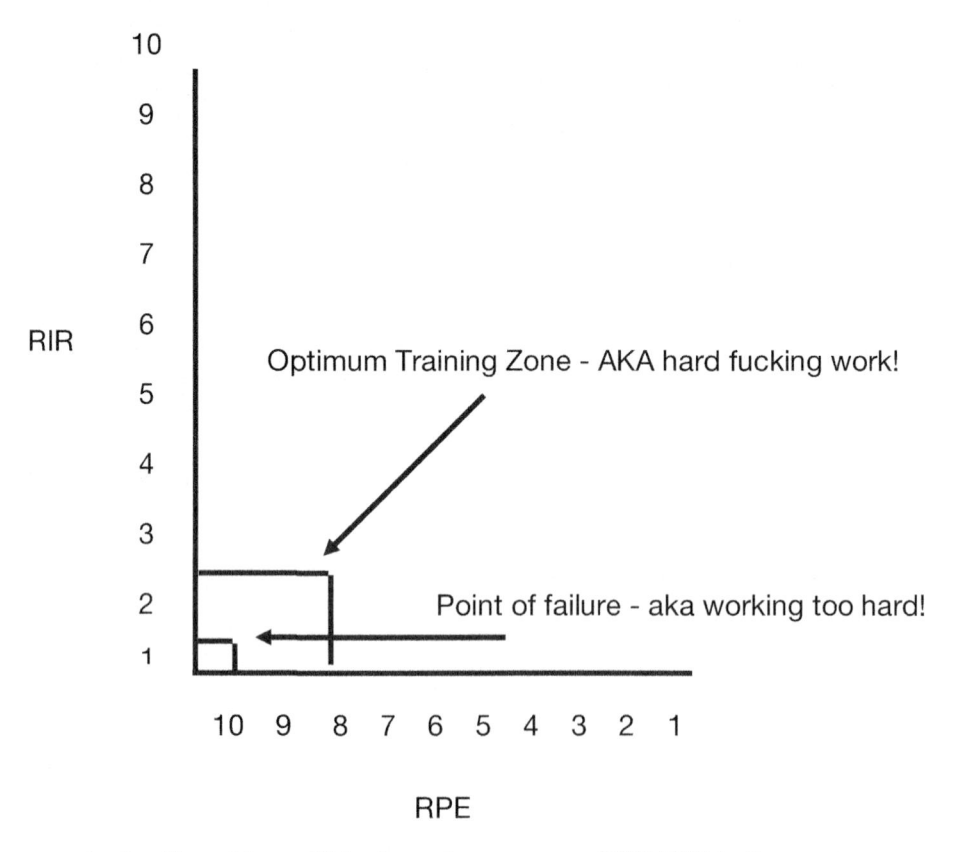

```
RIR
     10 |
      9 |
      8 |
      7 |
      6 |
      5 |        Optimum Training Zone - AKA hard fucking work!
      4 |                    ↙
      3 |
      2 |___
      1 |__|←——         Point of failure - aka working too hard!
         10  9  8  7  6  5  4  3  2  1
                        RPE
```

A significant benefit to focusing on your RPE/RIR is it removes the need to ego lift.
If you're unaware what an ego lifter looks like, next time you're in the gym take a look around, when you see the person who is clearly lifting heavier than they're capable of, with the most

questionable form you've ever seen, that my friends is an ego lifter.

Ego lifting achieves two things; A significant risk of injury and a significant reduction in results due to not actually training the desire muscles effectively.

You also look like a bit of a cunt, so my advice is to stop trying to go heavier than you can and focus on the effectiveness of your training, keeping good form and training to within 2 reps of failure. After all, we can all walk around like we have massive fucking bollocks making it hard to close our own legs but in the absence of enormous bollocks you're only kidding yourself.

When it comes to training volume you want to consider a few factors to ensure you're getting the most out of your sessions.

Frequency and intensity have been covered and the advice is simple, aim to train 3 times per week and hit each muscle group each week. Never train the same muscle group two days in a row and where possible have at least 2 or more days between training a set muscle group.

Aim for an intensity that enables you to hit your rep ranges without sacrificing your form and keeps you one to two reps from failure.

The volume, however is more about how much load you are putting the muscles through, how many sets, how many reps and how many exercises.

This will determine the rate of progress, and like the intensity and frequency will be governed by how often you can train as well as how long you have for each session.

When it comes to resistance training there is an effectiveness cut off that will vary for each person but essentially means that as you go beyond an hour, for some it might be more like an hour and a half, there will be a drop off in performance due to the fatigued muscles meaning the longer you train, the more exercises, sets and reps you do the less effectively you will be training by the end of your session.

Because of this it is worth looking to train for around 45-60 minutes, aiming for between 4-8 separate exercises. I would recommend around 2-4 working sets per exercise within a rep range that suits your goal. In short if you're not a powerlifter I would aim for between 6-20 reps per set.

Focus on maximising the main compound lifts first when you are most fresh as they will deliver the biggest impact and work the most muscle groups. They also require the most effort so prioritising them is great for maximising performance. After your compound lifts, targeting the muscle groups you're focusing on in that session I would recommend moving to some accessory lifts that target the desired muscles more specifically with isolation moves.
This will ensure you work the desired areas hard enough getting a good amount of volume.

In order to train effectively you want a good amount of volume each week to ensure you're fatiguing the muscles effectively to then stimulate the growth of new muscle fibres.

There are a number training splits you can adopt when resistance training. A good rule of thumb, if training 3 times per week is to aim for a Push, Pull, Legs split. You don't have to be training in this manner, but it does ensure each muscle group is worked with a great amount of volume each week.

Push, Pull Legs is essentially three sessions;

A push session focusing on push movements that target the chest, shoulders and triceps.
A pull session focusing on pull/row movements targeting the back and biceps.
And a leg session usually targeting quads, hamstrings, glutes and calves.
There are many other ways to split up your training, you can do upper and lower splits which may enable you to hit each muscle group twice per week.

For me, personally, I find I can get more volume into each muscle group, as well as getting enough rest and recovery between training each muscle group by going with a Push/Pull/Legs split.

As stated, though it is largely down to what you will enjoy the most, what allows for the most volume each week, effective recovery and falls in line with any specific aesthetic goals you have.

In summary, when it comes to training volume, intensity and frequency my advice would be this;

Resistance train 3-4 days per week.
Work each muscle group at least once per week, with at least 2 days between training muscle groups.
Aim for between 4-8 exercises per session, prioritising compound lifts first with accessory and isolation movements coming second.
For hypertrophy aim for between 6-30 reps.
For strengthen keep weight heavy and aim for 1-5 reps.
Work to an RPE of 8 and a RIR of 2.

If you can do that consistently you will make some great progress!

Programming.

When it comes to establishing your training plan, what you're going to train, how often, how many sets & reps and how often you change the plan, this is often referred to programming.

Effective programming plays a significant role in progress with regards to your training performance and seeking progressive overload.
However, due to the growing popularity of both body building and competitive powerlifting programming has become somewhat overcomplicated and difficult to get your head around.

So, allow me to simplify the fuck out of it for you.

When putting together a training plan there are a number of considerations to take into account;

How often you can train each week
What equipment you have access to
Ability
Your goals from an aesthetic and performance basis.

Once you understand your ability, what your trying to achieve and how often you can train it makes it a lot easier too structure your plan to maximise your efforts in the gym.

Something people get a bit confused about is how often to progress their workout and how often to change it and let's be honest, if you're competing in either powerlifting or bodybuilding then your programming probably needs to be bang on to improve on the lifts you're competing in or to improve the specific areas of your physique that might need more work.

For the average person looking to drop fat changing the program is less important. Why?
Because we get good at something through repetition. And whilst enjoyment is a key factor to long term adherence if you're constantly changing your program every couple of weeks it will be very hard to gauge your performance and therefore progress from a training perspective.

What is more beneficial is having a plan and sticking to it for 12 weeks, aiming to improve all your lifts in that time. After 12 weeks potentially switch the plan up a little in favour of a different training split, new exercises or just a different make up of reps and sets.

In truth there is only a finite amount of exercises for each muscle group so even with regular programming and changes to you plan you will probably find yourself doing very similar exercises. Think about it, anyone who wants to get good at anything will practice the same thing over and over and over. Tiger Woods doesn't constantly change his swing; LeBron James doesn't change his shooting style and Ronaldo or Messi don't change their free kick routine weekly. They practice the same thing over and over and over.

Your training is the same. You want the main compound lifts and some accessory lifts and to repeat and improve it every week.
There's a reason why the main compound lifts still form the foundation of all training programs even after centuries of advancements to equipment. Because they're the best and in reality, you just have to repeat them over and over to change your physique.

So, whilst you could look at the top strength and conditioning coaches, the top powerlifting coachers or top physique coaches and adopt their approach to your programming the reality is you will just be over complicating the basics.

For your goals of dropping fat, feeling happier, healthier and changing your body composition you just need a plan you enjoy that fits your lifestyle that you can stick to and repeat week in and week out allowing you to seek progressive overload over time.

You don't need to change it up every week or two or fuck around with the programming too much in terms of reps, sets, deload weeks or worrying about strength vs hypertrophy.

Just focus on working hard to an RPE of around 8, consistently each week trying to be a little better than you were the week before.

Does this mean every week needs to see improvements and the weights need to go up week on week?

No, because quite simply it won't. It doesn't mean your programming needs looking at, it's just a part of the process.

In short, when it comes to your programming and how fast you should 'progress' your workout you should be focusing quite simply on what's known as Progressive Overload.

Now this sounds scary but it really just means trying to progress your workout overtime. That progress can be more weight, more reps, more sets, greater control, less rest, higher intensity. But in short it means each time you train you should aim to do a little better than the week before. It doesn't need to be huge improvements every week, but ensuring you're training to the required RPE and pushing yourself a little

further than the last time will ensure you don't hit a training plateau and continue to make progress.
Something that is probably more important, and often massively overlooked, than your programming and how often you change the plan is rest, recovery and sleep. Something I am going to talk you through now.

Rest & Recovery.

A key factor in making progress comes from recovery. In fact, the majority of muscle growth happens at rest, when we are recovering.

And yet it is a factor many people overlook. All too often people try to train every single day, hitting each muscle group 2,3 or even 4 times per week and wonder why they always have injuries and progress is slow.

So, I am going to talk you through the best and most optimum rules of thumb for recovery to ensure you're maximising your efforts, because let's face it. No on, and I mean NO ONE, wants to slog it out day after day thinking they're going to look fucking insane only to end up actually slowing their own progress by not recovering properly.

Firstly, let's look at recovery and rest in the gym, between sets. How much is too much and how much is not enough so you can maximise efforts.?

This will be driven by your goals somewhat, if your goals are performance based your required rest may differ from someone with a more aesthetic goal.

Why? Because if you're looking to hit PB's on big lifts and build strength that discipline requires you to maximise each lift and be as explosive as possible so you can run as little risk as possible of failing the lift. Whereas if you're trying to change your physique, this requires you to fatigue the muscles and push beyond that feeling of fatigue and point of failure. This requires less rest between sets so that you can really push beyond that point of failure and exhaust the muscles effectively.

So how much rest should you realistically take between sets?

To make it easy I will split this into two groups, strength/performance goals, aka powerlifting, and aesthetic goals, aka everyone who isn't powerlifting.

Powerlifting is all about, as the name suggests, power. It's lifting as heavy as you can, with the correct form… this is not the same as ego lifting!
But when you're operating in rep ranges of between 1-5 trying to go as heavy as you can you need a lot of rest between sets. It isn't uncommon to rest for 5 minutes between sets. For many people this would seem too long but remember powerlifting isn't about training to fatigue the muscles. It's not about how good you look or having the most aesthetic physique. It's about building strength and being more explosive. Low rep ranges mean the weight is much heavier and therefore the most important element is recovering between sets enough to hit the next set.

It is better to rest longer between sets when powerlifting to actually gauge strength and stand the best chance of completing the lift.

Now, most of you aren't likely to be powerlifting and will be looking at achieving hypertrophy which results in muscle growth, muscle endurance and ultimately drives aesthetic and compositional change.

Traditionally it was believed that hypertrophy was achieved in rep ranges of between 6-12 reps with anything above that just delivering endurance.
We now know that hypertrophy occurs in rep ranges essentially between 6-30 reps and is all about pushing to the point of failure and beyond by fatiguing the muscles.

In order to do this, you want to take less rest between sets so the muscles recover enough to hit the next set but not so much that you're totally fresh to go again as you would want them to be when powerlifting.

The challenge is most people fall into none of two categories. They either rest too long because they're exercising their thumbs too much between sets or they all but skip the rest altogether and go from set to set without skipping a beat or pausing for breath.

A good rule of thumb for rest when resistance training is around 1-2 minutes. If you're able to go straight into the next set without any rest or only a few seconds, you're not lifting heavy enough and therefore not working hard enough in each set, or equally if the weight is quite heavy, you're not doing enough reps! You should need to rest between sets if you're training hard enough and effectively.

Similarly, you don't want each set to feel like the first set, you should be feeling more and more fatigued as you progress through the sets as ultimately, you're trying to fatigue the muscles effectively.

So, to summarise, when it comes to rest and recovery in the gym you want to aiming for 1-2 minutes rest.

Unless you're powerlifting in which case a minimum of 5 mins between sets is likely to be required.

That's in the gym, but how about rest and recovery, in general, outside of the gym and between sessions?

A lot of people have been fed a lie when it comes to rest, in particular rest days.
There was a social media mantra of #noexcuses and #zerodaysoff that led people to believe they need to be training every single day.
I am here to tell you that rest and rest days are very important.

In fact, I would say rest days are like arseholes. Whilst you may think they're just full of shit they're actually vital to how we operate and without them you'd end up in a lot of pain and discomfort.

But how much is too much, because I am sure a lot of people end up on a slippery slope to gaining weight through taking one too many rest days.
I once saw a video on social media claiming never skip three days of exercise in a row because;
One day we can handle easily.
Two days isn't so bad at all.
Three days won't hamper progress but you're now letting yourself believe that you don't need to exercise.
Now, I would personally break this down a little because for some people you might only be able to train on a Monday, Tuesday and a Wednesday, let's say. This would mean every week you'd have 4 days of no training in a row. This isn't an issue if your calorie targets are based around training 3 days per week.
What I would say is to not miss all three days of training though in a row as that is where the trouble can start.

It's not about not training when you weren't planning to train, it's all about not missing too many of the days you said you would train.

Now, before you think *"Hang on Paul, you said the #zerodaysoff mantra was bollocks"*. I sure did, and I stand by it. What I am saying is this;
You can have days off from when you were supposed to train. In fact, it will almost certainly happen due to injuries, illness and any number of unforeseen circumstances. This is fine and a part of the process. However, don't allow yourself to become lazy by missing sessions you deep down know you could have got in and if you do miss a session, or two… try not to miss three in a row.

Given rest days are important and not to be feared, how may is enough and how many is too many?

When it comes to training specific muscle groups you want to realistically give yourself a minimum of two days grace between sessions. Training the same muscle group on consecutive days can significantly reduce how effectively you perform and also increase the risk of injury. Two things you really don't want to do.

When you first start training it is really common to experience delayed onset muscle soreness, known more commonly as DOMS. Typically, this is worse, not the day after training but on the second day after and then progressively gets better. As your body gets used to training the DOMS gets much less noticeable. It's not because you're not working as hard it's just that your body and more significantly your muscles are more used to training and therefore recover better.

This doesn't mean you can or should train the same muscle group more frequently. In fact, when you're new to training and experiencing the worst DOMS ever, making every trip to the toilet feel like a military operation, you listen to your body and rest, stretch and recover not training that muscle group for 3 or more days.

This should be the same even when you don't really feel DOMS anymore. You should still give yourself a minimum of two days between training the same muscle group.

Whilst it may sound counterintuitive to rest and not train as frequently the difference in performance levels and subsequent progress that will be made aesthetically is significant enough to focus on training 3-4 times per day over training daily.
It also significantly adds value to ensuring adequate rest between sessions on each muscle group.

You want to maximise your efforts and get the most out of the gym so if that means taking rest days, then it should be embraced.

Rest days don't have to mean doing absolutely shit all though, active rest days are a thing. Doing things that you don't normally do and just keeping generally active on days out of the gym will ensure your activity level doesn't drop too much which is often what brings the trepidation and anxiety around resting.

For most people there's a fear that rest days means doing nothing and in resting all progress is lost. This just isn't the case; you can rest without being inactive and taking rest days will improve performance and progress of the sessions you hit and shouldn't be feared. Not least because the majority of our growth and recovery actually happens at rest. So, if you don't prioritise rest, you're also not prioritising growth, recovery and repair which will undoubtedly hold you back in the long run both aesthetically and from a performance perspective.

Another time where we rest that is very important to our progress is when we are sleeping, which is what we will be talking about next.

Sleep.

Sleep, much like hydration is one of the single most overlooked aspects of what will determine the rate of our progress.
All too often people overlook sleep and its importance and wonder why they're struggling to see the progress they're trying so hard to achieve.

Now, whilst sleep might be a commodity you have to do without, if you have young kids or work commitments that impact your general lifestyle which, in turn, impact your ability to sleep. It doesn't stop it being an important element of success.

Yes, you can still make progress without a huge amount of sleep, and some people perform very well on low sleep usually thanks to caffeine! That being said, if you can prioritise good sleep the benefits it brings are significant.

One of the biggest factors to good sleep is the positive impact it has on our mood and energy levels.
This carries huge knock on effects in your everyday life. With better mood comes a greater and more positive view of the world and ourselves. We have a way more positive body image and perception of progress when we are in a better mood.

Then we have the positive impact on energy levels, this helps us navigate the day way more effectively but more importantly it means we perform a fuck load better in our sessions. The better we perform the greater the progress! Plus no one wants to feel tired all the time!

Typically speaking the more energy, you have the more active you will be throughout the day as well, this is huge from a fat loss perspective because if we can increase our NEAT it can really boost our TDEE making it easier to be in a calorie deficit!
So not only does our training benefit but our general activity does too and as such so does our progress, massively.

Another significant benefit to sleep is the role it plays in our recovery.
The majority of our recovery happens at rest, we rest most when we sleep.
It is why things like poor hydration can ruin sleep because our muscles can't fully relax meaning our brain doesn't shut down, when that happens, we can't recover properly as well.
So, when we realise that most of our growth, muscle wise, and recovery will happen when we sleep it tells us a few things.
Firstly, it tells us that with good sleep the better our muscles will heal and repair, the better they heal and repair the better we perform when we next train and the better our progress.
It also tells us that the better we sleep the more muscle we will be able to build as well.
Which is why it is useful to have protein before you go to sleep to aid that recovery when our body is repairing most. Suddenly those *'don't eat after 6pm because it turns to fat'* folk are looking even more stupid than they did before, right?!
Anecdotally there is also a correlation between getting good quality sleep and the amount of calories we consume.

Now, whilst this isn't an exact science and correlation and causation are not the same thing hear me out.

And no, the link isn't that if you can't sleep, you're more likely to raid the fridge in the middle of the night, something I used to do as a toddler… I loved me some cheese in the middle of the night.

There is a common connection between those who suffer with low sleep and overeating. Why?
Well, simply put, if you're fucking tired throughout the day you're more likely to turn to more calorie dense food for a sugar hit to 'perk' you up a bit. You may also find yourself running off of those delicious caramel lattes, double shot coffee & double shot caramel, to get you through the day. This could be a huge factor for struggling to stay within your calories each day.

When we get good quality sleep and are actually well rested, we rely less on food and drink to carry us through the day meaning it is easier to stay within calories when in a deficit.

So, with good sleep we can expect to have better energy, better mood, better recovery and actually find it easier to stay within calories as we depend less on regular sugar hits throughout the day.

But what if you can't get good sleep due to health conditions or that STD that costs us the most… kids! (Just kidding, kids are great!)
Does this mean you're destined to be fucked?

Well, in short… no. Many of my clients have kids, some have health conditions that hugely effect sleep. Some work nights! All make progress because, whilst sleep plays a key role in how we feel, it doesn't actually dictate progress on its own.

The only thing that dictates progress is the amount of calories we consume daily over an extended period of time so, if like many, sleep is an issue for you this doesn't mean you can't see results.

Obviously, it is very beneficial to prioritise your sleep but if you're unable to improve it beyond where it is it just means greater emphasis on your overall nutrition is required to ensure good results and optimum recovery.

If you are someone who doesn't get a lot of sleep, I would ensure you eat enough protein to not only aid recovery as best as possible but to also keep you fuller for longer to help prevent snacking. I would also prioritise getting a good amount of carbs each day to help manage energy levels, especially before you train.
I would also recommend that if you do need energy drinks or caffeine that you perhaps opt for zero cal monster (other brands are available) so you can get that boost without adding a fuck load of calories to the day.

If nothing else, getting good sleep makes you feel happier and ensures you're a more pleasant person to be around as you have more energy and are less cranky. So, trying to get better quality and more sleep where possible is a really easy, quick fix, that can have a huge positive impact on your performance, recovery and progress.

In Summary.

So, when it comes to our training there is no 'one size fits all' approach. There are methods that carry greater benefits than others but the overriding factor to your training is enjoyment. What will you enjoy most, find that and so it because if you enjoy it, you'll actually want to do it.

The obvious caveat to this is that if you have specific aesthetic or performance based goals that require specific training approaches, in that case you will have to knuckle down and do what's required.

It doesn't matter if you do all the cardio in the world if you're eating more calories than you burn it won't do anything for fat loss.
Equally if cardio isn't your bag… there's no requirement to do it for fat loss.

In fact, cardio is great for building your baseline fitness level and heart health as well as increasing how many calories you burn but if you don't enjoy it… quite simply, don't do it.

Resistance training is great for increasing your energy expenditure both when training and at rest. It helps you add more muscle which means you burn more calories at rest as well as helping to prevent sarcopenia as we get older.

HIIT, despite what you may have been told, isn't magic or more superior than any other training styles… it also sucks dick in my opinion. People who like burpees and battle ropes need to have a long look in the mirror.

In short when it comes to your training ensure you are not trying to overcommit with what is possible. It is better to be honest and base your calorie target on training twice per week, if that's all you can do, rather than trying to go 6 times and failing.

Do the kind of training required for your goal, that you actually enjoy and just be consistent!

Try to progress your workouts so you don't fall into a training plateau and harm your progress.

Let's face it, your training, whatever it is, should be something you actually enjoy and find fun, if you hate it how the fuck do you ever hope to stick at it?

Section 3
Building Your Lifestyle

Results and Mindset.

Now, we have covered the two physical elements of reaching your goals and hopefully given you a decent view of what you need to physically be doing for your goals with regards to both nutrition and training.

Now it is time to turn our attention to the other element that will determine if you succeed with your goals or not…

Your mindset and how you track and monitor results.

Something that is worth considering is that most people quit on their goals, not because they failed but, because they think they have fucked up far worse than they actually have.

So, this section of the book is dedicated to ensuring this doesn't happen to you!

The 80/20 rule.

Something you may have heard me bang on about on social media, and I will absolutely hammer home in this section of the book is this delightful phrase;

"One hot day doesn't make a summer!"

Now, there are a few people who are from the North of England, Scotland or Wales who may well disagree, because that one hot day per year is their summer. But for the rest of us who have slightly less shit climates one day of sunshine doesn't constitute a summer.

What I mean by this is;
One day of doing something particularly well or one day of overindulging doesn't determine our progress. Moments in isolation aren't what define and dictate the results we get. Our results are driven by our consistent action.

Just like we wouldn't expect to eat one salad and drop a shit-ton of weight we can't allow ourselves to fall into the trap of thinking one day of eating increased calories is going to somehow ruin our progress thus far and damage our future potential.

It only becomes an issue if the exception becomes the rule.

Now, I personally don't preach a hardline 80/20 rule because I have some personal grievances around it but it is a good rule of thumb that if you're doing the right things 80% of the time 20% of the time you can enjoy yourself.

80% healthy and nutritionally dense food, 20% higher calorie less nutritious food.
The reason why I don't preach a hardline with this though is with some people there is a risk that if you give an inch, they will take a mile.

Tell someone they can cut loose 20% of the time and suddenly every meal is *'part of the 20%'*.
For some people they need a little more discipline and it looks more like 90/10.

The point still remains that when trying to manage your mindset you need flexibility. You need to be able to enjoy your life and not feel heavily restricted.

The phrase I often use is flexible dieting.

Aiming to average the right amount of calories over a 7 day period, rather than trying to hit the same number every day is just one simple mindset fix that can make an enormous difference to your progress.

Most diets preach perfection and have zero margin for error which, whilst beneficial for progress, leave you very unlikely to be able to stick to long term and almost impossible to actually enjoy and make part of your lifestyle.

Because let's face it avoiding all social situations and never deviating from the plan, avoiding all the food you love and being a slave to the plan for the rest of your life sounds fucking amazing… said no one ever!

But despite perfection not being a requirement for progress we still all too often convince ourselves we have be perfect and the minute we deviate, even a little, we think we have fucked up way more than we actually have.

Yet if we just accepted that sometimes we eat a little more, and sometimes we eat a little less, we would be able to stay on track a lot easier. We'd also find it much easier to get back on track after short periods of indulgence.

Most of the time people quit on their goals, not because they have totally fucked up beyond repair but, because they think they have fucked up worse than they actually have.
This is simply born out of trying to be too restrictive in their efforts.

Accepting that you can still eat the food you like, have a social life and indulge now and then relieves so much pressure and makes long term adherence substantially more likely.

When you adopt a long term mindset, instead of trying to do

something very restrictive for a few weeks you buy flexibility, you buy the ability to actually enjoy your life safe in the knowledge that having indulgences isn't something to avoid, it's actually part of the process.
The caveat to this is you still need to be consistent in your efforts. You still need to actually average the right calories consistently. This isn't the green light to be a gluttonous cunt until your hearts content. You do need to manage your calories the majority of the time to buy yourself the freedom and flexibility to indulge now and then.

Something that helps this is;
When adopting a long term lifestyle approach you actually can't fail. All that happens when you indulge is you slow the rate of progress. Understanding this is a fucking game changer for long term progress.

But this brings us back to the initial point. Accepting and knowing this is only a positive benefit to your prospects if you ensure your indulgences are the exception and not the rule.

Aiming to be on track for between 80-90% of the time and allowing yourself between 10-20% of your time to enjoy yourself not only ensures you will make progress it also ensures you will enjoy the process, not restrict yourself too heavily and still feel like you have a life. Adopting a lifestyle approach is the key to long term success. After all there is no benefit to adopting a short term plan for a long term problem.

The 'Fuck it' Button.

Now, I can guarantee we have all hit this at one point or another.
'The Fuck it Button' refers to that moment when you've just eaten something you perceive to be *'bad'* and you feel that instant guilt. That 'Hagrid' moment of *"probably shouldn't have had that"* which is usually followed by that sudden feeling of extreme recklessness where you think *'In for a penny, in for a pound'* and you hit the fuck it button.

This then leads to a virtually uncontrollable binge that can last anywhere from the rest of the day to maybe even a week!

Why do we do this? Well in truth, it is fucking simple. Almost all diets tell us that some foods are bad and to be avoided, so when we do finally cave in from our enforced restriction, we feel like we have totally fucked up which, once the guilt subsides, leads us to think there's no point in trying so we go all in.

The reality of this situation is that the perception that not only are some foods to be avoided at all costs, but also that the pursuit of our goals requires perfection are just false. They're ideologies that we will never ever achieve.
No matter how good your will and intentions you will never… and I mean NEVER achieve perfection. Life will always be a joyous little shitcunt and throw some curveballs in there you weren't expecting to throw you off track.

The trouble is, almost all traditional *'diets'* don't allow for this. They don't account for the fact that many things are beyond our control and even things within our control require an element of flexibility.

The pursuit of rigid perfection kills more goals than almost anything else because the second you deviate; you feel like you failed. You haven't, but you feel like you have!

So, what should you do when you indulge?

Enjoy it, draw a line under it and move the fuck on. Get back on track at your first available opportunity and you will be just fine!

No one ever failed to get results after six months of consistency all because of one bad day or week, as we covered in the last section.

In fact, to put *'The Fuck it Button'* into perspective, think of it way;

Hitting the fuck it button is a lot like reaching into the cupboard for a glass and you drop the glass. It smashes everywhere.
A rational response would be to clear up the mess, get another glass and go about your day. Sure, you're now one glass down but who counts their glasses, and you can always buy another.

The fuck it button, however, would mean that as that first glass breaks you think, *"Well, that's that ruined, might as well smash them all"* and you proceed to empty the entire contents of the cupboard onto the floor, walk away and leave the mess until you finally can't cope with it and attempt to clear it back up. Probably the next time you're thirsty, only to realise you have no glasses left because you acted like a fucking psychopath.

Now, tell me, does *'The Fuck it Button'* sound like a reasonable response to having one meal that was higher calories?

No, no it does not.
So, this is your sign that next time you indulge a little more than you perhaps wanted to, to not freak out and act like an irrational fool or petulant child by going way overboard. Draw a line, take a breath and carry on as normal and watch how much progress you continue to make!

Progress Tracking

Easily one of the most important things to get right is tracking your progress, how you track and what you track for progress will have a huge impact on your perceptions of your own progress.

In fact, most people think the main thing to track when it comes to their progress is their weight, they also think the best way to track is to check it all the fucking time.

I have sour news for you… **that is a recipe for disaster!**

Comparison is the thief of joy!

Constantly looking for progress will almost certainly lead to not seeing the progress you're looking for. Also comparing yourself to others will also do you absolutely no good whatsoever!

We covered weight loss vs fat loss already but given your weight is the most volatile metric, the most easily influenced and the one that gives a much less accurate indication of progress, it is also likely to be the one that impacts your emotional response to your own progress too it is crazy to think so many people only go by this and check it daily, sometimes multiple times per day.

I would argue the only times your weight is actually important is if you're doing a skydive our bungee jump and you want to ensure you're within the weight limit, you know… so the parachute or rope can actually hold you!

And if you check that shit daily, or multiple times per day, or week, you're literally going to end up pissed off more times than you are happy because that shit will fluctuate more than the British weather in summer time!

Similarly, if you're taking progress photos daily, or even weekly, constantly comparing yourself to others, asking friends how they're doing, looking at your favourite influencers regularly or doing anything other than what I am about to tell you, you will be setting yourself up for quitting.

Trust me on this, your progress will happen at whatever rate it wants to, all we can ever guarantee is if you're consistently ticking the right boxes the progress will come. How fast and where from is a little up in the air but it will happen!

No amount of comparing to others or constantly checking will speed it up or change that, it will simply leave you feeling like utter shit a lot of the time.

A watched pot never boils.

However, there is something you can do that will help!

Look for progress in the right places at the right times. With this in mind here is my definitive guide to tracking progress;

Track measurements of Chest, Waist, Hips and Thigh **ONCE** per **WEEK!** First thing in the morning, same day of the week, before you eat anything. You want to control as many variables as possible so doing it on an empty stomach, after going to the toilet first thing in the morning will mean your 'state' will be as close to 'the same' each time giving a much more accurate indication of progress.

Track your weight and take progress photos **ONCE** per **MONTH!**

Your weight will fluctuate, your photos won't change daily so don't look too often. Check once per month and notice the changes without getting pissed off with fluctuations or a lack of difference in photos.

Pay attention to how your clothes fit and feel! - if you're wearing smaller clothes, your current ones are looser, fit better and you feel more confident in them… that is way more important than what the scales say.

Listen to what other people say! If friends and family are saying you look good… they mean it! They're not blowing smoke up your ass!

Ultimately when it comes to progress and tracking your progress you want to ensure you're looking in the right places and comparing apples with apples.
Worry less about what anyone else is doing and the results they're getting. Focus on ensuring your measurements are moving in the direction you're wanting them to and remember, progress isn't just about the scales, in fact here are a number of things way more important than the scales.

Measurements - getting smaller? You're losing fat.
How your clothes fit - baggier clothes? You're losing fat.
Progress photos - see a difference between photos? You're losing fat.
Overall fitness level - feeling physically fitter? More important than what you weigh.
Strength - feeling stronger? More important than what you weigh.
Relationship with exercise - enjoying exercise more? More important than what you weigh.
Relationship with food - have better grasp on nutrition and less of an emotional connection to eating foods? Way more important than what you weigh.

Basically, focus on creating positive behaviours, routines and habits. Prioritise trying to improve a little bit at a time and guess what… the results take care of themselves.

Eating The Elephant

This next bit is called eating the elephant because it will be looking at how to actually structure your goals and what to focus on.

Sure, you may have 10kg to lose, or more. But simply waiting for the moment you hit that goal to celebrate is likely to be one of the biggest reasons you never actually reach it and is definitely a key reason why if you do, you won't stay there long.

Why do we quit our goals? More often than not, because we believe we are failing, not seeing results or have fucked up much worse than we actually have.

Making ourselves think that we aren't doing well enough is only going to end in quitting. But all too often we create an environment where the most likely outcome is feeling like we're failing.

Aiming to lose 10kg will delay all feelings of gratification and success for a long time. In fact, the goal should always, and only ever, be to lose the next **ONE.**
The next one kilo, the next once centimetre, inch, pound, whatever it is that you're monitoring.
Why just one?
Because, if you aim for the next one you could achieve that in the next week or two, meaning you get something to

celebrate almost every week. If you're waiting to drop 10kg that could be 6 months before you get to pat yourself on the back, meaning you have to wait a long time to feel like you're making progress.

Now, I want you to imagine you've been told you need to eat an elephant. (For all the veggies and vegans, please bear with me here, no actual elephants are about to be devoured).
If I asked you to eat an elephant the last thing you would do is attempt to eat it in one.
Jeez, we've all made the mistake of trying to eat a cake or biscuit in one go to find out it's a lot bigger than we realised. Now multiply that by 1000 and there ain't no way that elephant is being eaten in one go! Not even one sitting!

In fact, the way you would go about it is simple, you would cut it into bitesize chunks and eat it one bit at a time, for as long as it takes.

Your fat loss goals are the elephant and reaching them is you, eating the elephant.
Break that overall goal down into manageable bite size elements that are easy to focus on and achieve. Not only will you enjoy the process much more, you will have regular moments to celebrate and be able to see your progress so much easier!

And given than you're far more likely to quit if you feel like your efforts aren't paying off, it is incredibly important to make sure you can not only see your progress but you feel like you're moving in the right direction.

But what about the speed of progress?

Speed of Progress

Well, thanks to a toxic diet culture, many people believe you should be losing fuck loads of weight and inches in next to no time.
We've all heard the Peter Kay joke of *"14st in a day"* and sadly the industry has created an impression that fat loss needs to be fast and in huge amounts.
The trouble is this just isn't the case, it is also not realistic which means so many people, who are making great progress, end up feeling like they're not doing well because it's not *'quicker'*.

I am sure you've said this; *"I've only lost 1lb this week"*.
1lb a week for a year is 52lbs, I bet if I told you, you could lose 52lbs in a year you'd beg me to tell you how! For some of you there would be nothing left after that! And yet here we are in a society where losing 1lb is considered a failure.
Cheers Slimming World, ya cunts!

We have already discussed the sliding scale between progress and adherence and that the quicker the progress the harder it is to stick to. But when it comes to setting your goals being realistic with your expectations will play such a key role in your overall prospects for success.

Thinking you will drop large amounts in next to no time is a fucking expressway to failure. Instead of putting a restriction on your goals of adding a time pressure what you need to be doing is understanding this one very important point;

It is better to move at one mile per hour in the right direction than at 100 miles per hour in the wrong direction.

It's why I always preach slow progress is better than no progress, because it fucking is! Sure, we all want it like yesterday but fat loss, building the body of your dreams takes time.
Especially if you want to hold onto your results! The longer it takes the more sustainable the approach meaning the easier it is to hold onto the results you get. And let's face it, you're not losing fat so you can go and gain it all back again.
And whilst we would all love to be in shape by the end of the week the reality is, this shit takes time and no amount of making your life a fucking misery will improve your long term prospects.

What everyone overlooks is their long term enjoyment and the role that plays in reaching your goals and staying there.
So, instead of getting swept up in trying to lose as much as possible as fast as possible focus more on creating a routine and lifestyle you actually enjoy and can stick to long enough for it to become a part of your life, that also delivers the results you're after.

If you do that you will make progress but also not feel like you're having to go out of your way to do so. Couple that with adjusting your perception of what progress is and how fast it should arrive and you're creating a recipe for success that quite simply can't fail!

Yes, some days will be better than others, some weeks will be more on track than others, but this isn't a social media highlight reel. This isn't a competition prep or aggressive cut for some good before and after photos. This is your life and in the real world you actually want to enjoy life whilst making progress so to do that we need to be realistic.

In doing that you will achieve far greater success than ever before as well as be able to hold onto it a fuck load easier, which after all is the overriding goal.
To improve your health, fitness and drop fat for the long term, for the final time and not to just yo-yo once again!

A significant part of managing the rate of your progress is actually enjoying the process itself.
If you enjoy the elements that will bring success, the success takes care of itself. If all you give a fuck about is the progress or end goal, I can guarantee you will hate it and quit long before you reach your goals.

"He who enjoys walking will travel further than he who likes the destination"

To put it simply if you have a process that you enjoy and can focus on sticking to, ticking the right boxes, implementing the right behaviours you will do far better than someone who's only focus is the end goal.

That is because when it all boils down, progress is the result of repetitive and consistent action.
No one, and I mean no one, is born instantly great at something. Anyone who has ever achieved anything, fat loss or otherwise, has done so by being consistent in their efforts and actions.

Kidding yourself into thinking you can achieve your goals with minimum effort, consistency and in an incredibly short timescale is beyond foolish.
After all, it didn't happen overnight that you ended up in a situation where you needed two make change. So why would you ever expect to be able to achieve progress in next to no time at all?

So, when it comes to the making lasting progress and managing your mindset and expectations, setting realistic time frames is essential for your own success.

Factors Of Failure.

There are going to be a number of factors or limiting beliefs that will play a role in our success, but also increase our chances of failure.
These factors and beliefs are often self imposed and more often than not dressed up in our heads as things we think will serve to help us.

Your own confirmation bias will be a significant factor in your own success, or failure. We often tell ourselves what we want to hear and seek out information to affirm that.
When we aren't seeing progress, we rarely look at our own behaviours to identify if in fact we could be doing more. We often look to external factors beyond our control to try and make an excuse for our lack of consistency.

Be honest, I bet you have said something like this, in response to being inconsistent with your efforts;

"Perhaps I'm just allergic to bread as if I eat it, I just bloat and put on weight" whilst also ignoring the fact you haven't been training properly and as well as eating some bread you haven't tracked calories for 2 weeks.

It's unlikely that the one day of including bread caused a huge spike on the scales or halted progress. But it's easier to blame something else than say *"I could be doing better"*.

In fact, so many people continuously pick shit diets, because they *'worked'* before. They don't want to have to spend time doing what they know is right so try to convince themselves that diet you failed at, because it was fucking shit, will be ok this time round.

Like always returning to that toxic ex, you find yourself trying to convince yourself *"it'll be different this time"*. It turns out it won't be!

But you continue to buy into the things that back up your own beliefs and ignore anything that suggests otherwise.
Ideally you need to drop all emotional attachment and bias and use data to guide your decisions.

Something that can make it harder to succeed and easier to fail is the input of others. Friendly fire if you will.

It's not just your own confirmation bias you're fighting against. Many PT's and professionals, as we explored earlier, will have their own approach based on *'what worked before'*. These opinions often positioned as fact often come from a good place but can make your chances of success smaller, if that approach isn't right for you.
What's worse is when that method doesn't work, rather than that person accepting their method may not have been the best fit, often the blame is put back on you and it is seen as something you're doing wrong rather than the method not being fit for purpose.

It's not just professionals though, friends and family members can also push their own confirmation bias and beliefs, often limiting beliefs, onto you.

We've all heard it, and I'll talk about it again later too, *"Should you really be eating that?"*

Or the classic *"I've been doing this diet and the results are amazing, you should try it"*.

Friends and family will always give their opinion, not because they want to sabotage you, they clearly don't, but because they have seen some success or have a perception of what progress or dieting looks like to them and they feel the need for you to conform to that view.

It is often from a good place but can be a huge factor in why you find it hard to find the right approach for you.
After all, two people can do the same diet and achieve very differing results.

Then we have the simple fact that people will often feel threatened by your actions and efforts and it's not uncommon for people to channel that into an attempt to sabotage your efforts.

As humans we seem to see other people doing well, trying harder and succeeding as a threat. We look at ourselves, doing much less and rather than take inspiration and ultimately taking action, we seek to bring down the other person.

You will never be negatively judged by someone doing better than you.

Unfortunately for a lot of people when they start doing well their friends and family may see traits in themselves, they don't like but rather than address that they will seek to bring you down to their level.
Perhaps not explicitly by telling you to stop, but don't be shocked if they keep suggesting drinks, or meals out, offering

snacks and sweets. It's not that they don't want you to succeed, it's more that they just feel shit about themselves and it's easier to slow you down than to begin doing more for themselves.

Another area that can really impact your progress and chances of success is another trick of the brain called Sunk Cost Fallacy.

This, in short, is where you allow the amount of investment in something to determine if you stick it out.

So, you may find yourself always going back to Slimming World or always cutting carbs because it's what you've always done.

You are more likely to continue doing something that isn't working than change tact, especially if you've been doing something a long time, even without success.

I once had a chat with a Slimming World member who hadn't lost weight, in fact had gained weight, over a six month period. But rather than accept it wasn't working for him and identify why. He just kept going. This is because it worked before and he'd invested so much time and money into it he felt obligated to keep going. Even though it was having the opposite effect.

We do it with our jobs, we end up in a job we hate for so long because the security of having an income is deemed better than finding something new.
We accept that because we have been there so long that it's better to stay than to actually try to be happy.

I can confirm, it is not better the devil you know.

Dieting is no different. Simply reverting to the diet, you have always done, or sticking out at something you know isn't working purely because of how much time and or money you have invested into it will never lead to results.
And whilst you may believe you're making a rational decision based on what you're set to gain from the experience, the likelihood is you're actually allowing your emotional and time investments accumulate making it harder to abandon something that's not working.

The harsh reality is, there will be many factors that can influence and impact on your progress. Many are out of your control but a good chunk are very much within your own influence.

Ensuring that you're adopting the right approach for you and making decisions from a place of clarity, based on research and data, rather than acting on impulse and emotion will always lead to you standing a better chance of success.
A key element to this is appropriate goal setting.

Goal Setting.

Now, we have spoken about progress, the speed of progress, measuring progress and even breaking things down into manageable chunks.

All of which are essential components to success and managing your mindset.
Something that is an absolute cornerstone to success is being able to set your goals effectively.

Goals should be easily broken down into Long Term, Mid Term and Short Term.

Your progress will run through phases, you will likely see a large amount of success at the start that begins to level out and plateau. You will likely then see a resurgence before arriving at a point where you reassess and often set new goals.

The truth is, we never really reach our goal and just stop. The closer we get to our goals the more we begin to think about the next goal.
In business we have milestones we wish to hit and often think *"It'll be great when we hit X"* It could be income, customers, followers etc. But in reality, when you reach that milestone, you're already focused on the next one.

It's why setting goals is important as fuck, but so is recognising achievements along the way. But how do we do that? Simple, you set goals you're going to be able to achieve.

As I said when talking about Eating The Elephant, breaking stuff down into manageable chunks gives lots of opportunity

to celebrate and keeps you feeling like you're making progress and moving forwards.
It shortens the window between goal setting and goal achievement known as delayed gratification.

When setting goals, it makes sense to have them split into time scales but it is also sensible to have regular reviews of progress but also if those goals are in fact still your goals.

What you may feel you want achieve in the next five years could be very different today to what it is in even six months' time so taking the time to reevaluate your goals is essential to long term success.

Short term goals should really allow you to form the behaviour patterns needed for long term success. They are quick wins, low hanging fruit and ways to build positive momentum. Rome wasn't built in a day and to reach your goals will take time, so breaking goals down into actions and behaviours required to succeed means you can give yourself specific tasks to complete each day, fuck even down to each hour if you like, that will add up to create the environment from which success can be achieved.

Mid term goals are a little more aspirational and often the result of the accumulation of your short term behaviours. These give the accountability and reason to keep doing the smaller daily tasks. They're close enough that they're in reach but far enough away that you have to keep going.

Long term goals, well these are way off into the future, they require not only the daily actions to be delivered consistently but also to meet each mid term milestone too that all add up to the overriding goal.

Breaking your goals down like this allows you to navigate the process, knowing where your efforts are best placed at all times.

One thing we often fail to account for is the dreaded plateau.

Plateaus will happen. It's a given. It doesn't mean what you're doing is no longer working or needs changing though.

Many perceived plateaus aren't actually a plateau at all. With fat loss we will navigate periods where not much changes for a few weeks here and there. It's part of the process.
When adopting a deficit that says you will lose on average 1lb per week, that doesn't mean you will lose 1lb each week. It simply means if you do it consistently for say 6 months, the total loss will equate to roughly 1lb per week.
It could come off at regular intervals, or in peaks and troughs. For most people they confuse this with being in a plateau when really, they just need to keep doing what they are and trust the process.

A genuine plateau usually arrives as complacency kicks in or if we experience a little set back or failure.

We get used to continued success and progress and then it slows or stops and we panic. The trouble is, if you become desperate, you're likely to mess everything up.

We make drastic changes based on emotion and irrationality and can allow our fear of failure to ultimately throw us off track.
Instead, if we have genuinely plateaued for a few weeks we need to step back and reevaluate.

Are we working as hard as we think?
Have we become complacent?

Could we be doing something differently?
Taking time to assess the situation and find the best practices for moving forward is essential for navigating and ultimately coming out of a plateau.
The answer is rarely that we're failing or unable to get results anymore. It's all too often we began to gradually ease up as the complacency that comes from sustained success began to settle in.

Again, having short and mid term goals allows us to look at what we're doing and why to ensure we're actually still creating an environment for success.

So, when setting our goals in general we need to ensure they are SMART.
Apologies for anyone who has a business studies GCSE but it is important to be sensible with goals setting as it is the goal setting that sets up the success.

SMART refers to Specific, Measurable, Achievable, Realistic and Time Related.
Ensuring our goals are specific, have a way we can measure how we're progressing, are actually achievable, aren't unrealistic and have a time frame attached is fundamental to success.

That applies to all goals, short, mid term and long term. If they are lacking in any of those areas then it is likely you won't hit them.

It is also worth noting that Parkinson's Law plays a key part here too.

Parkinson's Law, for those who are wondering what the fuck I am chatting about is this;

"The time allotted to a task is the time it will take to complete it"

Now, yes, there is a caveat, simply giving yourself an hour to do something that will take a year means you won't achieve it. But from a fat loss perspective you're likely to find that if you give yourself a short window you may well achieve it in that time but you will likely hate the approach.
So, when setting your goals be realistic, assess how likely you are to stick to and enjoy the required method to achieving the goals you set. Because if they're too ambitious you will make your life hell and you may not want to do that.

So, when you're setting your goals just remember to be SMART, and whilst we're dropping GSCE business studies content also remember this nugget of wisdom;

The 7 P's

Proper Planning & Preparation Prevents Piss Poor Performance.

And to round it off with a classic David Brent-ism
"To fail to plan is to plan to fail".

Ultimately your success is down you setting your goals in a way you can actually achieve them. It's not about being overly ambitious and kidding yourself into thinking you can achieve huge results in no time.

How you approach your goals will ultimately determine if you will reach them.

Something many people believe they need to be a success is motivation, which is exactly what we will look at now.

Motivation vs Discipline.

Now, for many people the belief is you need to be motivated to start and that motivation will drive you to your goals.

Often people look at those doing well and think *"How the fuck do they stay so motivated?"*.
Here's the thing. It isn't motivation that is keeping them so consistent. It is something entirely different.
It's discipline.

When motivation is in short supply, discipline is the behaviour trait that will keep you on track.

So, what's the difference?

Motivation is typically a short term mindset. Something that comes in waves and something that won't be there every single day.

No one wakes up at 5am in the middle of the winter and thinks, I can't wait to do a sea dip, go for a run or get in the gym. But many people do all those things almost every day. This is because in order to be consistent and get results you have to do some things you might not be all that excited about.

Yes, at the beginning you will be motivated and excited to start but that feeling may not last forever. It will peak as progress does but ultimately it will come in waves and there will be way more days where you feel like you don't want to than you have days where you can't wait to.

This isn't me preaching a #zerodaysoff or #noexcuses mantra here, don't get me wrong.
It is simply me pointing out that you will never be motivated every single day. And if you rely heavily on feeling motivated to take action the reality, is you will probably not reach your goal.

Inaction kills more goals than failure and waiting for motivation to peak will lead to a lot of inaction.

So, what can you do?

Be disciplined. On the days you don't feel like it, get it done.
I always hear the phrase;

"The best workout is the one you almost didn't do"

And this does ring true getting a session done you didn't feel up for will have you feeling great!
This isn't me saying drag yourself in when you're unwell, in desperate need of rest and just simply unable to train.

This is me saying that when you're not *'feeling it'* on a day you know that you need to take action, be that train, getting steps in or taking calories, the key to you getting results is making sure you still do those things. Make actions not excuses.

Something that makes it easier is, as I said, creating a routine that isn't too demanding! When it is easy to stick to and you

enjoy what you're doing you'll find your discipline is a lot better.
After all, no one skips doing something they actually like and want to do!

But when it comes to your goals and achieving the consistency needed for success the behaviour trait that will have the biggest impact is actually your discipline rather than your motivation.

Yes, having a strong *'Why'* is key to aid motivation, monitoring progress too but all that counts for very little if you can't trust yourself to actually tick the right boxes consistently.

There will always be days where you can't wait to do the right things but there will probably be far more where you kind of can't be arsed. It is on those days that you have to ensure you're ticking the right boxes because those are the days that will determine your results and the speed of those results.

One last thing that we have to take into account, from a mindset perspective is how we navigate certain situations we want to enjoy.

How To Navigate Social Situations.

Something that always threatens to throw a spanner in the works is what to do around social situations.

Now, we have covered a lot of how to approach it from a mindset perspective already but it's not just about how we view it mentally that is important to our success. A big factor is how we actually approach these situations as well.

The big three social situations that require the most important approaches are;

Your birthday.
Any holiday you're going on.
Christmas.

Outside of these there will be weddings, other people's birthdays, celebratory meals out, date nights and much more in between.

How you navigate these situations is critical to your success. To aim to simply avoid them is to commit to failure, or creating a life you hate.

But being a little too cavalier with them can also spell trouble so how is best to tackle them?

Well, I'm going to start with the big three first.

Your birthday is not a day for you to be *'on a diet'* for. If you're like me you have a birthday week, maybe even a month of celebrations if it's a significant birthday.
This is all fine, but will take some navigating.

Obviously for the day itself and I would argue a day or two around it, if your birthday isn't on a weekend, I would strongly advise that you don't diet. You don't open MyFitnessPal, you don't track. Just be present with your friends and family and celebrate! After all it is one day and it's a day all about you so enjoy it!
Once it has passed you simply settle back into routine and guess what? Nothing bad happens and you still make progress.

What about a holiday?
Let's face it, you're going on holiday for a break from the norm. You're not going abroad to just live out your usual routine in a warmer climate.
Whilst away training, dieting, tracking should all be left at home. You drop it all off at the airport as you leave and collect it again when you get home.

After all, no good holiday story ever started with a salad and no one wants to hear how good your training session was whilst away. They want to hear about the cocktails, the pool, that amazing meal and the memories you made.

Yes, you may put some weight on doing this for a week or two but want to know a secret?
That weight will be almost entirely water weight meaning after a few days of being back on track you will shed that water weight and be back to the pre holiday condition in no time. And so, what if you do gain a little bit of fat, it's worth it. You can always get back on track and work off the holiday weight. You can't go back and remake the memories you missed out on. So, enjoy yourself whilst away and get back on track once you're home.

Then there's the dreaded C word. No, not cunt or cancer. I mean Christmas.

My message here is simple. From Christmas Eve until Boxing Day switch off, don't even think about dieting or tracking. Just have the best time with your family.
If that means whiskey for breakfast and eating 11,000 calories then fucking have at it. After all, it's Christmas!
What we don't want to do though is begin saying *"Fuck it, it's Christmas"* from mid November, like many people do.
Try to stay consistent through December, yes, we may not be as perfect due to the social commitments and parties but ensure you do the very best you can from the 1st until the 23rd and then from the 24th until New Year you can relax and enjoy.
Much like holidays, no good Christmas story started with a salad and so what if we gain a little over the festive holidays. Having the best time with family is way more important than being able to say you stayed within calories. After all, enjoying yourself is what Jesus would have wanted, on his birthday.

That's the big three, what about all the other little events, meals, parties etc. that will crop up throughout the year?
In truth, if there's not too many you could adopt the same approach and just not track for it. We know one hot day doesn't make a summer so why stress too much?

If it's a little more common or you just want to stay on track a little better you can do the following.

You can either;

Plan ahead, pick what you will eat and drink in advance and track it so you know what calories are left for the week.
This will allow you to have what you like without going over, but may mean poverty calories for a few days to balance it out.

You could opt for the low calorie option. Sure, if you actually want to eat the low calorie option this is a great way to stay on track. Swapping to low cal drinks with zero calorie mixers, opting for the lighter meals are all ways to go out and not go over.

You may opt for something higher calorie that you want and swap the sides to lower calorie sides to minimise the impact. Another great option for managing your calories and eating what you like. Swapping Coke to CokeZero, swapping chips to a salad can all help save calories and make room for some of the food you like.

Or you have whatever you want, enjoy it and just get back on track the next day. Yes, you may go over but if it's a bit of a one off, who cares?

But how do you track food you're not actually making yourself?
Again, there's three options here;

You can search out the restaurant and dish, because many larger restaurants are on MyFitnessPal. This means what you track is about as accurate as it gets.

If they're not on there or you're at a friend's house you can either search out the name of the dish, for example 'Lasagna' and then pick the one that looks accurate. Don't pick the lowest calorie one though as I promise you, making MFP look good will only mislead you into making misinformed decisions further down the line. It's better to overestimate what you ate than underestimate.

You could log each element of the meal individually, guessing roughly what you had of each. This will help you track fairly accurately but is a little time consuming.

Anything that helps you track the food will ultimately give you a more accurate indication of where you actually are, which helps make better choices further down the line.
But sometimes we want to just eat and drink what we like and not think too much about it or feel too bad.
In that case I would say to not track at all.
If it is just one meal that's missing it won't make a huge impact in the grand scheme of things. Like we said about that one hot day and all that jazz. Not tracking one meal in isolation isn't the thing that will have a huge say in your long term progress.

In short, when it comes to those social situations you need to be able to enjoy them, if your diet doesn't let you, it's not a diet, it's a prison sentence.
How you navigate it is down to what will work best for you but remaining consistent outside of these social situations is what buys you the flexibility to actually enjoy your life and still make progress.

In Summary.

When it comes to your results, your mindset is the most important thing to protect at all costs.
Managing expectations, knowing when and where to look for progress and setting realistic goals are essential to your long term prospects.
Couple that with a plan that you can actually enjoy and you're well on your way to success.

You need to become focused on the process not the outcome and trust that through the right actions you will get the desired results.
Striving for consistency and not perfection and not freaking out when things don't always run smooth are absolute cornerstones to lasting success, and enjoying what you're doing.

Realistic timescales, with lots of easy to reach milestones along the way will have you feeling good and seeing progress all the time making the entire process easier to enjoy.

In short, your goals will take time and require you to do the right things. That doesn't mean it has to suck a bag of dicks. Creating a routine, you can enjoy and stick to whilst coupling that with realistic goals and expectations will see you will not only smash your goals but maintain the results too.

Trust me when I say this;
Going about it this way will always be way more enjoyable and long lasting than trying to do something you hate until you give up.

Diet Culture vs the 'Anti-Diet' & Toxic Diet Culture.

You might think this is an odd time to tackle this in the book and that it would be better placed in the nutrition section but hear me out.

Dieting and results are all about mindset and now you know the fundamental elements that underpin all successful diets, the calorie deficit, the importance of training for enjoyment and the way to manage your mindset it is the perfect time to unpick the diet industry in detail to ensure you know how to spot bullshit a mile off and what kind of approach you should be creating for yourself.

Before I get into each element in detail allow me to give a quick explanation of what these things are;

Diet Culture - the overriding culture of the diet industry that creates many of the misconceptions we all believe we need to adopt for results.

Anti-diet - the complete opposite of diet culture that promotes total food freedom. In principle a liberating approach but much like all things… often goes too far the other way.

Toxic Diet Culture - the toxic charlatans and zealots taking myths and misinformation, adding a side of pseudoscience to completely mislead you for financial gain. This usually ends up completely fucking up your relationships with food in the process. Usually coupling that with suggesting that one particular approach is better than all others and that any other approach is bullshit.

Now, you know what each of these things mean let's dive balls deep into them and explain what they mean to you, what's helpful and what you need to ignore and avoid like the fucking plague.

The reality is that these 'cultures' are everywhere. Not just on social media but these approaches form the basis of opinions for almost everyone. People you work with, friends, family members... literally everyone.

And because of that people around you will always have their own opinions on how you should be going about reaching your goals and what works best.

99% of these people mean well but are terribly misinformed, meaning their 'helpful' advice is fucking bullshit, and to be ignored at all costs.

Think about it, as I said earlier, I guarantee you've heard someone say;

"Should you be eating that" or

"I've started doing this diet and you should too"

This is code for, *"I have no fucking clue what I'm talking about but allow me to throw my pointless opinion at you"*.

When it comes to Diet Culture, it is fair to say that since the 80's and 90's diet culture has become fairly popular in the media, only accelerated by the emergence of social media. Now, all magazines, newspapers, and social platforms are a wash with stories and posts about various diets.
It has led to the diet industry being a multibillion pound industry and many a shitcunt wanting their slice of that dollar.

There is one overriding factor that runs through every 'diet' that gets glamorised. They are all about the speed of results. Essential these diets are simply trying to find out what crazy thing can you do to get fast results.

Usually endorsed by celebrities, who probably haven't done that diet but let's face it, it's all about keeping their names in the media and staying relevant so if you have to claim you drank donkey jizz to get in shape for a movie role you may as well.

The trouble we encounter with diet culture is it's not an accurate reflection of how to actually elicit fat loss.
Almost every glamorised diet, slimming club and product out there does one thing very very well.
They keep you from realising that the key to your goals is to bring yourself into a calorie deficit.
By doing this they can bring you into one without you knowing, creating an unhealthy dependency on their *'method'* in order to get results.
Whilst doing this they also simultaneously enforce false beliefs about what you can and can't do when trying to lose weight. They will demonise and glorify foods to back up their method which in turn actually damages relationships with food and the general understanding of nutrition for those who follow it. What's worse, this is not just whilst following it but potentially forever thereafter.

The reality is, as I've already explained through the book, is there is no right or wrong, good or bad way of creating a deficit. The best way to create one is the way you will enjoy and be able to stick to most. The method that brings about the least change to your current lifestyle to make the process of not only achieving results easier but maintaining them too is often the one best suited to you. Because, after all, fat loss isn't about losing it to regain it, it's about losing it for good.

So, when diets and the diet industry position such short term approaches and restrictive methods that they know you will never stick to, they're doing it to entrap you in a yo-yo culture and create a dependency on their approach.

The impact this then has on you long term is that your relationships with food are severely damaged. You end up creating fear, guilt and shame around certain foods. You create a thought process of I can't and shouldn't eat that which only worsens the all or nothing type approach.
It also ruins your perception of progress; what progress looks like and how fast you can expect to make progress.
The risk with this is when you adopt a more appropriate method for yourself you will end up believing you're failing not because you're not making progress but actually because you're not making it quick enough.

How fucked up is that, that you will make yourself feel shit for not making progress fast enough. You will overlook the fact you're making progress all because someone has led you to believe you could be doing it quicker.

It's this reason that a lot of people quit. They believe they're not doing well enough when in fact they're doing very well, they've just been sold a lie by the diet industry of what *'results'* should look like.

Basically, diet culture will have you believe that you have to restrict yourself to a place of unhappiness you could never hope to stick to in pursuit of progress at a pace you could never hope to achieve and when you don't achieve it the blame falls on you.

And trust me, this isn't even the toxic element yet! That's just diet culture in general.

So, surely the 'Anti-Diet' movement is a good thing, right? Well, kind of. The trouble is, like everything, people take things too far. What started as a campaign for more intuitive eating and just being mindful of calorie intake has now become a campaign for absolute food freedom and ignoring everything that can even remotely linked to dieting.
It has become an anti-calorie control movement where people will openly debate or dispute proven science because it no longer *'fits'* with their views and opinions. Remember what we said about confirmation bias?!

So, rather than taking the logical approach of adjusting opinions to meet fact, people are attempting to change the facts to meet their opinions. Which, I am sure we can all agree, is fucking stupid.
Not only does it not change the fact, it actually also stops people being able to actually apply the truth in a way that works for them.

Now, whilst calorie counting may not be for everyone, that's fine. After all it's just a method for monitoring intake to ensure you're in a deficit. What we can't get away from is that the only way to elicit fat loss is through a calorie deficit. So, whether you track or not, you still need to control calories one way or another. Something the 'anti-diet' approach is losing sight of.

One positive from stepping away from traditional diet culture is that it promotes more food freedom and let's face it, if there's one theme that's been consistent in this book it's doing the stuff you like. Eating the food, you enjoy is critical to success with any goal because you're not going to avoid the food you love forever.

Just don't take that too far, you can't expect to eat completely free of consequence, especially if what you're eating is particularly high in calories!

What's interesting is as we explore toxic diet culture there's elements of both diet culture and anti-diet culture heavily present and this is because the very toxic culture comes from people adopting an extreme stance of a belief or approach.

It's become completely normal it seems for people to straight up lie about a number of things to do with fitness and nutrition in order to push a very strict way of doing things.

The emergence of people promoting the carnivore diet, extreme versions of keto, fasting, even promoting veganism from a position of health superiority.
There's been the excessive hype of insulin management, demonisation of sugar, carbs, even protein has copped a bit of stick recently.

The thing is for every *'you should only do this'* shitcunt, there is another equal and opposite shitcunt saying the polar opposite, so who's right?

More often than not, neither of them!

There is no reason to go to extremes with your diet. Mass elimination of entire food groups is never a good thing. In fact, many of the very extreme opinions are tantamount to disordered eating rather than actually being an appropriate and recommended way to create a deficit.
The reality is our bodies are complex things that require a wide variety of vitamins, minerals and macronutrients to function properly.

Encouraging the removal of large swathes of these, fuck yeah, I just used the word swathes, is nothing short of dangerous. So how do they get around this?

Two very important things are done to gloss over how dangerous this advice is.
Number 1 - the citing of very questionable research or studies that aren't applicable to human behaviour or real life. This is done to sound credible safe in the knowledge you won't do your own research on the subject.

Number 2 - The use of pseudoscience and misinformation to sound clever and knowledgeable on a subject. It makes the theories sound plausible and again there's a lot of hope put into the fact you won't go and check this stuff out.

What's particularly toxic is that the people pushing these ideologies and this misinformation are actually generating large followings, more and more people are beginning to believe that what they're saying is true.
Not only is that actually dangerous from a health perspective but, it means that more and more people are now outright denying fact because it doesn't provide the confirmation bias needed to keep their dicks hard over whatever shit stain approach they have adopted as gospel.

This is fucking dangerous because if we allow people to continue to deny the facts and position their opinions as truth it pushes people further from the truth and means people are making more and more decisions that will be at a detriment to their overall health.
It further damages relationships with food, relationships with health in general and ultimately means more and more people will be putting themselves through unnecessary and overly restrictive routines for absolutely no reason.

If there is one thing that I want everyone who reads this book to take away it's that in the pursuit of your goals I want you to never again do something you wouldn't actually enjoy doing. I don't want anyone to ever get caught out by misinformation and be led to believe something that simply isn't true.

If, through reading this, you can learn to spot when someone is chatting shit and you can easily identify the best way for you to create a deficit, to live a well balanced and all round healthy lifestyle then I will consider this book a success.

In life we know how to look after our homes, our cars, how to hold down jobs, look after our pets but we have a piss poor understanding of how to look after our bodies.

Currently as it stands, we only have one body and one planet to live on and if we fuck both up beyond repair it's going to be pretty shit. Now, I can't do a lot about the planet… and this book isn't about climate change.

But I can help you to better understand how to look after your body. Regardless of your goal, I can ensure that you're actually doing the stuff that's important and not making your life harder than it needs to be. That's what this book is about.

"But how do I know you're not actually one of these toxic diet culture extremists?" I hear you ask.

Well, good question, the reason you can be sure I am not is think about the message I have kept through this book.
I haven't dictated you must only do x, y and z. I have broken down the science behind your goal and given advice on how to apply that. But at all times I have maintained that the key is taking that information and applying it in a way that YOU can stick to and enjoy long term.

There is no *'you must do this and only this method'* just a simple explanation of what the principle behind your goal is and the guidance to apply that how you see fit.

Some of you will skip breakfast and call it intermittent fasting. Some will reduce carbs; some will try to limit fast food. But the key is, whatever method you adopt you will be doing so because you understand the reason for doing so rather than being led to believe that is the only way to do it.

That is how you can be sure that I'm not another toxic diet culture shitcunt trying to keep you at arm's length from the truth.

So, we have really covered all the important elements that will guide you to your goal.
We have looked at Nutrition, Training, Mindset and a deep dive into the diet industry.
The only thing left to do is look at how we take this and apply it moving forward.

Section 4
This Is Just The Beginning

The Takeaway!

No! I don't mean that kind, but as you will now know, they're fine in moderation, and encouraged too as part of a long term approach.

What I want you to take away from this book is the key elements behind your goal.

When it comes to fat loss there is one principle that governs it, a calorie deficit.
The best way to create one is to do so in a way you will actually enjoy and can stick to long term. No amount of will power will have you sticking at a diet you hate. None whatsoever!

Like anything in life, something worth having takes time and effort and fat loss is no different. But when the approach is right it won't feel like hard work and can actually be enjoyable. That's why it pays to adopt a long term lifestyle approach.

After all, no one gains fat overnight so we can't expect to lose it quickly, especially if you intend to keep it off and I am sure you're not losing fat just to gain it back.

When it comes to exercise the key is to do what you enjoy and be realistic. Don't expect to go from never training to training every single day overnight and keep that up.
You may well want to incorporate resistance training for so many reasons, not least it will drive the actual change to your physique.

Lastly, steer clear of any pseudoscience, toxic diet culture bullshit that encourages adopting overly restrictive approaches and demonises certain foods.

Your life is for living and your diet and exercise should add to your quality of life and not take away from it!

If you feel you're struggling then there is always the option of joining my Academy, The ReDefine Academy.
In there you will find everything you need to be a success. You will have programs to choose from, your calories calculated along with your protein targets, support, accountability from yours truly and my team of top tier coaches. There's a community, for added supports, a recipe library full of hundreds of recipes for added inspiration and an ever growing video library covering all topics that will get you success.

Basically, in one app you will have everything you could ever need to be a success, there's even an option to go pro and work with me or one of our coaches 1-1.

I wrote this book with the view of giving you all the information you need about fat loss, that is relevant and worth knowing.
I didn't want to overwhelm with more information than is required, big old scientific words and making it all seem incredibly daunting.
The industry does that enough as it is.
You google fat loss and you're met with a million different views all neglecting to tell you the underlying principle of what actually matters. A calorie deficit being the only way to elicit fat loss and the one thing every diet seeks to create.

You have got this book, this tool, forever at your disposal. Everything you could ever need is right here.
But remember, this book isn't another PT launching their shitty diet book on you. This isn't a get fit quick scam designed to sell copies whilst dressing up a calorie deficit with bullshit workouts and a shitty meal plan that only looks good

thanks to spending a small fortune on photographers to make the meals look great.

No, this book is designed specifically to enable you to navigate this world without falling for the bullshit and without getting swept up in anything that isn't a concern for fat loss.

But this book really is just the start.

Many of you will read it and enjoy it and go on to implement the guidance in it for yourselves and I think that is fucking great!
However, many more of you will do what you have always done, and therefore get what you have always got… you will fail to put into practice what this book has taught you.

After all, we're all guilty of it and I am sure you have done it a million times before with self help books.

The issue, you see, isn't exactly a lack of information or access to information. The issue is that you struggle to apply that information in a way that works best for you.

It can be pretty overwhelming knowing where to start and how to apply everything you have just read, in a way that works best for you.
That is exactly why this book is just the beginning.
For those who are happy to implement this themselves, it's the beginning of you starting your journey and finally reaching your goals, becoming a success and keeping the results long term.
It is the start of changing your life, for the better, for good.

For those needing a bit more help, well this book is the gateway to the next step in your journey.

The first step in what I know will be a very successful journey we are about to take together.
This book is the insight into what my academy is all about. It is the confirmation you needed to take action and join my academy.
It is step one on the road to the best version of yourself.

The self sufficient and self starters will have this book for company along the way.
For those who need a little more help, you will have something even better.
You can have me, alongside you for as much of your journey as you wish.

Imagine having me, helping you to understand each element of this book, helping you to implement it in a way you can enjoy and stick to and coupling that with all the support and accountability you could ever need to reach your goals.

Well, that is all achievable within my academy. Not only that, there's countless video modules covering many of the topics in this book, and more as well as the recipe library and not to mention your own programmes to know exactly what to do, to apply everything in this book to your own lifestyle.

There's also the community of people just like you, who have been where you are and took that first step and never looked back.

It may feel like you're about to do a sky dive, but think of it this way. A sky dive with an instructor is much easier as you're not the one who decides when to jump.

So, why don't you let me take the stress out of everything and guide you safely to your goals?

Now, I reiterate, this isn't a typical diet book. This book is your sign to take action. It's a message to yourself to finally take the first step towards a new you.

Who knows what you can and will achieve in the next few days, weeks, months and years. The reality is, you're in full control of how it all plays out.
I can't predict the future but I can confirm that if you take the right action, you can and will achieve everything you could ever imagine.

What comes next for you is entirely in your hands and what you do once you turn the last page and put this book down will directly impact what's to come.
With that in mind, it is a massive thank you from me, for getting this far and entrusting me to guide you up until now. For those going it alone, I am wishing you every success and just know I am always happy to help.

For everyone else, stood nervously at the edge of your journey deciding when to take that leap, let me take that jump with you.

The final page of this book is by far the most important one for you.
Turn to it, you'll know what to do from there.

Thank you once again for reading.

Paul.

Acknowledgments

I feel it is very important to take this moment to give praise and thanks to the people who helped make this book what it is.
Without a select few people I simply wouldn't be where I am today and this book simply couldn't have happened.

Firstly, I want to thank my clients past and present, and those who are yet to join. It was a fucking daunting prospect leaving the corporate world of sales to embark on this journey, and I remember laying in my garden writing my first ever business plan, dreaming of being where I am now.
Every single person along the way, from those I helped for free to get some experience, to the first bunch of Paul Andrews Fitness members, to the face to face clients I worked with across multiple gyms and to the members of what is now called The ReDefine Academy. From the bottom of my heart, I am grateful for each and every one of you. You have all taught me so many lessons in life and business and allowed my dream to become a reality.
Each person has left their mark and I am eternally grateful. Without all of these amazing people I quite simply wouldn't be where I am, so thank you all.

Then we have the absolute foundation of everything in my life. My Wife and family.
The support shown by Kelly and my family over the years has been immense. Sure, they probably all would have recommended going about my journey slightly differently and in a less cavalier kind of way, but I am sure deep down they knew I'd be alright.
Without Kelly I don't think I would have made it through the ups and downs of running my own business quite so well, her support and encouragement has been critical to my success,

not to mention how she carried our household through the pandemic, which very selfishly arrived just 3 months into my first year as a fully self employed coach!

Life can be a bit of a cunt at times and without the love and support from Kelly I am sure I wouldn't be where I am right now, I'd probably not be here at all. I am very lucky to have her and incredibly proud to not only call her my wife but honoured that I get to love her and call her my best friend.

Then there's my family, my Mum and her husband Johnny have been incredible to me. I know my mum worried every day in the early years of my business, she probably still does now to be fair but through the worry their support and encouragement to chase my dreams has without doubt got me through.

My Dad has helped me along the way, his experience of running businesses and building them from the ground up has helped me no end, his support and knowledge has guided me without question.

Marc, my brother, deserves a mention too. Not so much for the years of torment when growing up but potentially for the concussion caused when recreating WWE for knocking the sense out of me enough to not be scared to give this shit a go! But also, because having been in the same industry before me and left he never tried to discourage me, instead shared what he learned from his success and failures to help make my business a success.

A big mention also goes to my best friend Roxy. We've known each other since we were born, well since she was born, and after years of our parents forcing us to be friends, we're now best mates through choice and see each other off our own backs. Roxy gave me the push I needed to go self employed, coupled with the likelihood I might just be out of a job if I didn't quit. But without her believing in me enough to convince me to believe in myself this journey may never have started!

It is without doubt worth thanking Otto, of Otto House Coffee Shop. For two years I went in every other Wednesday to spend time writing before a trip to the barbers. This book was almost exclusively written sat by the window, on table 3, drinking their coffee. Without their chilled vibes, Otto's chats with me each time I was there and their amazing coffee this book would have taken even longer to write!

Lastly, I want to thank Megan, my social media guru, manager and mentor.
Megan was originally a client of mine. In the beginning we began exchanging services for each other to keep costs down. She helped with my Instagram, I helped with her goals. It soon developed into a very fundamental part of my business. She has helped me through multiple website launches, a full rebrand to the academy, the launch of the app and also was chief proof reader on this book.
I don't know how many times she will have read each section but I know for a fact without her keeping on at me each week this book may never have been finished.

Every person has played a role more significant than they could ever know and I am incredibly grateful.

So, from me, to all of the family, friends, clients and peers;

Thank you.
Paul

Recommendations.

Here's a few recommendations of fellow peers within the industry that have helped me along the way both personally and through their content, who I personally endorse for sharing decent, evidence based information.

James Smith @jamesmithpt
Ben Carpenter @bdcarpenter
Martin MacDonald @martinnutrition
Jay Alderton @jayalderton
Graeme Tomlinson @thefitnesschef_

Remember where I said to turn to the last page?
This is why.

If you enjoyed this book and feel like you need a little more help along the way, with your journey then head to The ReDefine Academy and join today.

ReDEFINE. ACADEMY

Paul Andrews Fitness
Personal Trainer and Nutrition Coach

www.redefineacademy.com

@paulandrewspt

Printed in Great Britain
by Amazon